3.9.77

The Folklore of the British Isles
General Editor: Venetia J. Newall

The Folklore of Wiltshire

The Folklore of Wiltshire

Ralph Whitlock

Drawings by Gay John Galsworthy

ROWMAN AND LITTLEFIELD
Totowa, New Jersey

First published in the United States 1976
by ROWMAN AND LITTLEFIELD, Totowa, N.J.

ISBN 0-87471-772-8

Printed in Great Britain

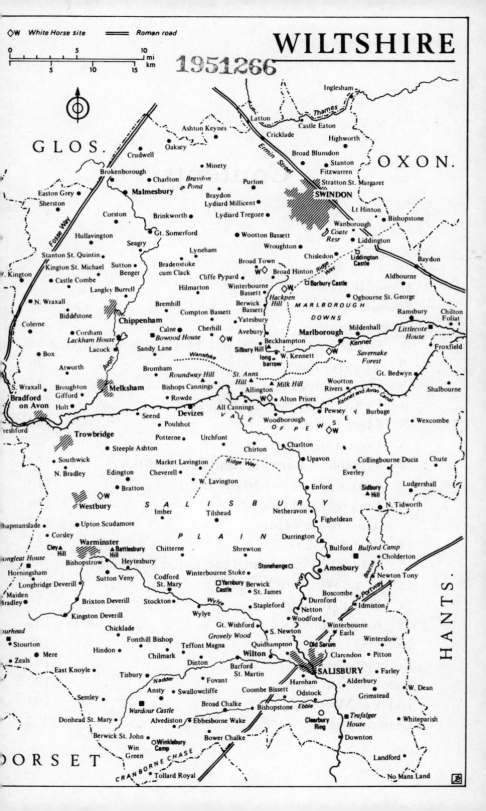

WILTSHIRE

◇W White Horse site ═══ Roman road

1951266

Contents

Foreword

Wiltshire's outstanding monument is, of course, Stonehenge.
Layamon called it the 'giant's ring,' and Thomas Middleton
(1580-1627) referred to the 'Hanging stones in Wilts.' John
Aubrey (1626-97) linked its construction with the Druids – for
in his day they were thought of as the first educated Britons –
fulfilling the role which earlier writers had assigned to Merlin;
the label stuck.

Stonehenge does not consist of hanging stones, and it was
not built by giants; nor was it ever really a 'very Temple of the
Winds,' as Thomas Hardy called it. Indeed, its original
purpose predates both the Druids and the legend of Merlin.
But all these picturesque titles became part of a tradition, and
so for the folklorist they have acquired a certain validity. Even
the idiosyncratic, when it derives from or contributes to a
general mood, or to wider concepts, cannot be dismissed as
irrelevant. Aubrey would have endorsed this view, for he loved
to gossip, and he would have recognised that the universal
may often be explained through the particular. The reverse is
also true.

Born in a remote and lonely part of west Wiltshire and
raised among peasants whom he regarded as 'Melancholy,
contemplative and malicious,' Aubrey longed for knowledge of
human experience. This led him to relate antiquities to the
everyday life from which they came. He shared the
fashionable antiquarian enthusiasm of his time, but this
broadness of outlook marks him out as the first genuine
forerunner of the 19th-century school of English folklore.

The Victorians reflected his enthusiasms. They shared his
regrets, and these attitudes became more pronounced in
20th-century followers of the same school. Aubrey held the
Civil Wars and Commonwealth responsible for the great gulf
dividing the good traditional life of former times from the
spiritually impoverished period in which he wrote. He
lamented the disappearance of the 'Roman or Arcadian
Habit' worn by Wiltshire shepherds – 'a long white Cloake
with a very deep cape which comes down half way their backs,
made of the locks of the Sheep; their Armature was a Sheep
Crooke, a Sling, a Scrip, their Tar-box, a Pipe (or Flute) and

their Dog. But since 1671, they ... goe à la mode' – presumably because it was cheaper or more practical. Today folklorists recognise that traditional behaviour and belief survives or disappears for genuine reasons and, further, that the process itself is of interest.

Edith Olivier, a modern devotee of old Wiltshire life, wrote in terms similar to Aubrey during World War II: 'A black-out is the true emblem of the Nazi onslaught. It substitutes for Nature's ringing of the changes the dull roar of aeroplanes overhead: the autumn weed burning and the Guy Fawkes bonfires must give place to the horrid glare of fires destroying homes, churches and hospitals.' Aubrey, in the same way, was naturally saddened by the destruction which the Puritans caused. But the disappearance of shepherds' cloaks and bonfire customs is another matter. Folklore is as much a part of change as it is of tradition. When a custom is discontinued or adapted, the underlying reason, as well as the actual change, should be our concern. So often this is not recognised. About ten years ago, for example, a correspondent in Aubrey's part of Wiltshire described local bonfire customs to a folklorist. The Guy Fawkes tradition was elaborate and centrally organised before 1939, but 'Gradually this deteriorated – fireworks, especially squibs, are the main attraction, there are bonfires in several places (or even none), and only a few children are interested anyway. War and the money for fireworks are accountable.'

When a belief or custom is interesting, attractive or amusing, or if it serves a socially cohesive purpose, we regret its passing. But aspects of new folklore are also welcome for identical reasons. Unidentified Flying Objects – and Ralph Whitlock provides an informative chapter about them – are a good example. Here is an instance of war contributing to folklore, since enthusiasm for the phenomenon was stimulated by sky-watching during World War II.

Ralph Whitlock brings to his subject a true understanding of tradition. He was born and bred in Wiltshire, and spent most of his life there. He is a real countryman, with a genuine appreciation and a critical insight into the subjects which he covers. His book is a most welcome addition to this series.

London University   Venetia Newall
August 1975

Introduction

WIDESPREAD LITERACY has been a feature of English life for less than two hundred years. In Pitton, the Wiltshire village where I was born and where I spent much of my life, I remember a fine old gentleman, a thatcher, who wrote with exquisite copperplate handwriting, but it took him about a quarter-of-an-hour to sign his name. He read slowly, his finger following the words along the lines.

That was in the 1920s. He must have been one of the first products of the village school, which, still admirably functioning, was built in 1853. Prior to the 1870s there is a marked deterioration in the quality of handwriting in the marriage section of the parish register. The farther back one goes the worse it is, until in the 1840s many of the girls were unable to sign their name. 'Keziah Collins – her mark', wrote the parish clerk, and alongside it Keziah inscribed a rough cross which looks as though it were made by a pen held tightly in a clenched fist.

It must never be assumed, however, that illiteracy is synonymous with a lack of intelligence – those eighteenth-century peasants and labourers, and their ancestors, were as bright as we, their twentieth-century descendants. What they lacked was opportunity. In my boyhood I knew many men and women who could barely read and write, but I never thought of them as unintelligent.

An intelligent illiterate man has fewer distractions than we have. He is better able to focus all his powers on the problems on hand, be it an exercise in craftsmanship, or how to get the better of his neighbour, or the truth about an abstruse point of theology, matters uppermost in the minds of some of our forefathers over at least three or four centuries. Add to the limitations of illiteracy the restrictions on travel that kept most of our rural ancestors confined to within a few miles of their birthplace, and we are confronted with a powerful concentration of human intellect.

The memory of an illiterate man, uncluttered as it is by masses of half-digested reading matter, often strikes us as phenomenal. Many nineteenth-century cottagers possessed only one book, the Bible, which they read very laboriously, were able to recite long sections of it by heart. They remembered the ditties, songs and legends learned in their youth, and they in turn passed them on.

One such, which stems directly from the Bible, says that 'Adam were made and then put up again' a wold (old) hurdle to dry'.

Others concentrated on craftsmanship. In my early teens I learned from a near-illiterate man how to make a rick of sheaves. Every sheaf had to be handled correctly and placed correctly. There was one pattern for the outer layers of sheaves, another for the inner ones, and making the roof was a very complex matter indeed. But under my exacting taskmaster I was able to fashion ricks that stood erect and kept dry in the winter storms.

An interest in folklore was natural to me. I was born in the village of Pitton in 1914 and spent my boyhood there in a time when we had no piped water supply, no telephone, no electricity, no sewage system, no daily papers and, of course, no radio. My memories go back to the carrier's cart, which used to take two-and-a-half hours to travel the six miles to Salisbury. Some of the villagers, particularly the women, visited the town only twice a year – at Easter and in October for Salisbury Fair. I remember seeing the first car to enter the village; the first plane to pass overhead.

Both my father's and my mother's families had lived in the village for centuries. There are Whitlocks on the first page of the parish register, in about 1650. My father and mother were married in 1901, but I, their first child, was not born until 1914, when both of them were nearing forty. So, by the time I arrived, my parents were fairly set in their ways. They tended to live, to some extent, in the past. Conversation was often of old times, or people whom they had known and of what they had said and done. I absorbed a great deal of folklore without being aware of it.

We were small farmers. I left school at sixteen, in 1930 when the Depression was at its worst. Soon afterwards I started writing for local papers, for the sake of pocket money. In 1932 I began a column of country notes for the *Western Gazette* and its associated papers, which circulate throughout Wessex, centring on Wiltshire, Dorset, Hampshire and Somerset but extending into Devon, Berkshire and Gloucestershire. This column I have written, week by week, ever since.

Among the main sources of material for this book are my personal reminiscences and the correspondence connected with my weekly column in the *Western Gazette*. In it I write on any country subject, but folklore is a favourite. One joy of the work is that readers provide at least half of the material. My correspondence is voluminous, and a tremendous amount of information has been collected over forty-two years.

Much additional material has accumulated through my other activities in the county, in connection with the Young Farmers' Clubs, the local Natural History Societies and in the compilation of BBC programmes. I used to know Miss Edith Olivier, that grand pioneer of Wiltshire folklore collection, and from time to time I exchanged notes with her.

Of the original material in my possession one of the items which pleases me most is the story of the Odstock Curse, (page 135). It was given to me in the late 1940s, and I wrote a radio play around it. The story concerns events that began in about 1801. The Curse itself was pronounced at an unrecorded date, but probably between 1810 and 1820. In the 1870s the Odstock blacksmith, Hiram Witt, wrote down his recollections of the events, and the story is given in his own words.

Back in the 1930s I learned that the village of Martin (now in Hampshire but earlier in Wiltshire) was the original of Winterbourne Bishop, the downland village of W. H. Hudson's *A Shepherd's Life*. I often stayed in Martin and got to know many of the villagers, who knew Hudson, including the lady with whom he lodged when writing the book.

'He made a lot out of nothing,' one old farmer told me. 'Old Isaac Bawcombe, as he called him . . . that was old Lawes. I minds him well. Knew his shepherding well enough, but a bit of an old fool otherwise, Well, 'sno, he used to tell a yarn about there once being a big city, with seven churches, up on Martin Down. That'll show ee what a fool the old chap were.'

My informant, whose family had lived at Martin for centuries, knew nothing about a city on Martin Down. Yet at Rockbourne, the next village down the valley, the late Mr Morley Hewitt subsequently spent several decades uncovering the foundations of a Roman villa so extraordinarily spacious and elaborate that it must have been something special. It is suggested that this may have been the Imperial Stud Farm in Britain, the estate extending for miles around and including Martin Down.

So was 'Isaac Bawcombe' simply using his imagination, or had he heard a garbled recollection of a time when there were fine marble buildings in the vicinity, albeit a mile or two from Martin Down? It seems perhaps unlikely but not impossible. The dim past used to be known locally as the time 'when there was a king in every county' – a not inaccurate description. On page 107 is a ghost story of phantom horsemen near Pitton which could be a folk memory of a time, before the reign of Queen Elizabeth I, when horsemen rode that way to mediaeval Clarendon Palace. This shows how the centuries can be bridged.

On the other hand, allowance has to be made for imagination and fabrication. An old man, living within six miles of Stonehenge and obsessed, like many people, by the problem of how the stones got there, assured me that they had been brought to the site 'bucket by bucket'. In other words, they were made of concrete. When I objected that stone was very different from concrete, he retorted that they had had a secret method of making concrete in those days, to make it look like stone. Not only is the idea preposterous but I doubt whether it was even a tradition. I think it originated in the old man's head.

Wiltshire has a better than average share of prehistoric sites and monuments, including Stonehenge. Predictably, they have legends attached. But how much importance should we attach to those legends? Did any of them originate in the ages when Stonehenge was relatively new? In view of the pertinacity of oral tradition among illiterate people, it seems a possibility. On the other hand, the legends may have appeared at any subsequent date. The one concerning the

Devil (page 17) could be mediaeval.

Nor, as in the example of the old man and his concrete, can we often be sure whether a legend is genuinely old or whether it has been made up in comparatively recent times, the product of whimsy or exuberance. The association of Stonehenge with the Druids, which one hears from many people living in the neighbourhood, is almost entirely due to the imagination of certain eighteenth-century antiquaries.

In the following pages I have dealt first of all with the prehistoric monuments – Stonehenge, Avebury and the downland barrows. I then go on to the hill sheep fairs, which seem to have had their origin in prehistoric times. The hill carvings, mainly of white horses, suggest antiquity but probably belong to much more recent times.

Then follow chapters of festivals, which cover the rural year. There are more local customs, a chapter of traditions concerning places, and another which deals with characters and personalities. Wiltshire, (see Chapter 9) has large numbers of ghosts, apparitions and other supernatural curiosities. Chapter 12 – Animals, Plants and Traditional Remedies – deals mainly with personal recollections, though material from literary sources is included. Many of the beliefs recounted are still widely held, and the dialect names for things animate and inanimate continue to be used. The concluding chapter concerns folklore in the making, and here I have included the Warminster and other Unidentified Flying Objects.

Since its formation in 1853 the Wiltshire Archaeological and Natural History Society has published in its Magazine many items of county folklore. In the 1920s and 1930s Miss Edith Olivier began gathering information about local customs, legends and other memories from village Women's Institutes; her first collection was a little paperback book, *Moonrakings*. Much of this, together with additional material, was published in her later books. In the 1950s the Wiltshire Women's Institutes along with those in other counties started their own collections, and each Institute was invited to compile a Scrap Book of local information. Most of these are now kept at the County Library in Devizes. Most deal primarily with current affairs at the time of the compilation of the book, but some contain much interesting history and folklore. And some of the Institutes followed up their efforts by producing a duplicated history and miscellanea of their area. These are invaluable sources.

Kathleen Wiltshire, who has lived since 1940 at All Cannings, in the centre of the county, has been collecting folklore and memories from the Institutes and other sources. Her *Ghosts and Legends of the Wiltshire Countryside,* published in 1973, is a mine of information.

Of early Wiltshire collectors the first and most distinguished was John Aubrey, whose surname perhaps derives from Avebury, or Aubrey as it was sometimes called. His *Natural History of Wiltshire* was written, in the form of disconnected essays, between 1656 and 1691, though they were not collected together and published till 1847.

Aubrey was among the first to associate Druids with Stonehenge, a fancy which was taken up and embroidered by almost every antiquarian who wrote about Wiltshire in the next two centuries. John Smith, John Wood and Dr William Stukeley are outstanding examples.

In the second and third decades of the nineteenth centuries Sir Richard Colt Hoare, of Stourhead, compiled his monumental *Ancient History of Wiltshire* and *Modern History of South Wiltshire.* His 'Modern' Wiltshire has now become moderately ancient, and his book therefore supplies an invaluable background to life in the county one hundred and fifty years ago.

When county and town guide books came into fashion, the earlier publications concerned themselves very little with folklore and concentrated mainly on architecture, scenery and history. More productive are somewhat obscure volumes dealing with certain localities. One which I enjoy is William Chafin's *Anecdotes and History of Cranbourn Chase,* 1818; for much of the Chase, as originally defined, lay within Wiltshire.

Finally, I should like to express my sincere appreciation for the courtesy and cooperation shown by Mr K. Lloyd Plumridge and the staff of Yeovil Library, by Miss R. Greene, curator of the Wiltshire County Library, by Mr Roger Kneebone, stock co-ordinator of the Wiltshire Library and Museum Service, by Miss Jane Butterworth, of the same Service, and by the many informants who, by word of mouth and letter, have provided material over the past forty years.

1 Stonehenge, Avebury and the Downland Barrows

IN THE HEART OF the chalk downlands are the great megalithic monuments of Stonehenge and Avebury, the colossal earth pyramid of Silbury, and a galaxy of barrows of all types. The downs are crisscrossed by ancient green trackways. The hilltops are crowned by quietly impressive earthworks, now grass-grown. For reasons now forgotten, men of the past dug deep trenches and threw up massive ramparts; one, the Wansdyke, runs right across the shire.

No written records of the origins of these features have survived, if indeed they ever existed. Nearly everything published about them is conjecture, and, until very recently, it was based on exceedingly flimsy foundations. In the present century, excavation and investigation by modern methods have increased our knowledge.

Most remarkable of all, perhaps, is Professor Gerald Hawkins' contention that Stonehenge is so accurately locked on the apparent movements of the sun and moon as to form a very reliable calendar. Having made and checked all his calculations by a modern computer Professor Hawkins demonstrated how Stonehenge itself can be used as a computer, for predicting eclipses and similar phenomena.

It is necessary to add that his theories have been the subject of considerable controversy and criticism, though I for one find it less difficult to accept than to fault them. If he is anywhere near the mark, our respect for the achievements of our prehistoric ancestors must be greatly enhanced.

Traditions and legends connected with sites like Stonehenge and Avebury are of two types. We can differentiate, or at least attempt to differentiate, between what local people say and what early scholars have written. In the case of Stonehenge, it is quite likely that some of the local oral legends derive in part from written records.

In the official guide book to Stonehenge Professor R. J. C. Atkinson, writes: 'Stonehenge is unique. There is nothing like it anywhere else, and from the earliest times it has aroused the awe and curiosity of its visitors.' He is probably right, but the awe did not extend to local folk. They seem to have simply regarded Stonehenge as part of the scenery. I was born within ten miles of the site, and my father in his early days as a shepherd followed his sheep on the neighbouring downs long before barbed wire or motor traffic existed. We heard only one Stonehenge legend, which I will shortly tell. I remember being taken there to picnic as a small boy, in our first car during the early 1920s. We sat on the stones and played around them. There was no-one else in sight, on all the vast grassy Plain. It was a pleasant place to visit, with nothing awesome or sinister about it. I remember the hundreds of rabbits scampering over the close-cropped turf.

The local attitude towards the 'hanging stones' is probably typified by the activities of 'Gaffer Hunt of Ambresbury', recorded by Dr John Smith, an eighteenth-century worthy who wrote a highly imaginative book about Stonehenge while staying at Boscombe following an inoculation against smallpox.

'Gaffer Hunt,' says Dr Smith, 'built a hut against the

upright stone of Mars; and attended there daily with liquors, to entertain the traveller, and show him the stones. His cellar was under the great stone next the hut.'

It is a homely and realistic touch among all the fancies about King Bladud, the Hyperboreans, Boadicea, Divitiacus, the Druids, the Fomorians and other characters real and imaginary known to antiquity. Gaffer Hunt, showing off the stones to travellers, may conceivably well have told them the only oral legend I have heard from residents in villages nearby. This is what it says:

Stonehenge was built by the Devil in a single night. He flew back and forth between Ireland and Salisbury Plain, carrying the stones one by one and setting them in place. As he worked he chuckled to himself, imagining the surprise of the local inhabitants when they awoke next morning and saw what had happened.

'That'll have 'em puzzled', he boasted. 'They'll never know how the stones came there.'

But a friar was lurking in a ditch nearby, watching all. When he heard the Devil's boast he could not resist exclaiming, in broad Wiltshire,

'Ah! that's more than thee ca'st tell!'

The Devil, startled, dropped the stone he was carrying into Bulford Brook, where it can still be seen, immovable.

In his anger he picked up one of the largest stones he could find and hurled it at the friar, who was, naturally, running away, and so the stone only struck his heel. The mark can still be seen today on the Heel Stone, which stands, isolated from the main structure, by the edge of the road.

The friar, and indeed the story as a whole, suggest the Middle Ages. The stones are the work of the Devil and the friar, representing the Christian Church, gets the better of him; this implies a recognition of the site as in some way hostile to the new religion. Another interesting detail is that the stones came from Ireland. Most of them, the sarsens, were almost certainly fetched from the Marlborough Downs, in north Wiltshire, but some, the so-called blue stones, came from farther afield. The nearest place to Stonehenge where this type of stone is found is the Prescelly Mountains, in Pembrokeshire; hence it is generally assumed that this was their source. Indeed, over fifty years ago, Dr Herbert Thomas of the Geological Survey showed this to be so, and it was later supported by the discovery that the central Altar Stone, though of different type, probably came from the same area.

It is by no means certain that the story of the Devil and the Friar is an authentic piece of orally-transmitted folklore. For we find what seems to be the germ of the story in the *Histories of the Kings of Britain*, written down by that highly imaginative romancer, Geoffrey of Monmouth, in the twelfth century.

Geoffrey begins by quoting, with liberal embellishments of his own, a tale evidently read in the chronicles of a ninth-century writer, Nennius. It concerns Vortigern, king of Britain in the years after the departure of the Roman armies, and Hengist, one of the early leaders of the Saxon invaders. Hengist persuaded the British nobles to attend a peace conference, unarmed, and then treacherously massacred them all.

Geoffrey offers the additional information that the massacre occurred at Sarum, 'on the calends of May', and that the number of 'earls and princes' who had their throats cut was 460. After the ineffectual Vortigern had disappeared from the scene, he was succeeded by a stronger leader, Ambrosius Aurelianus, who is supposed to have given his name to Amesbury. One day at Sarum Ambrosius remembered the nobles who had fallen and 'was moved to pity and tears began to flow. At last he fell to pondering . . . in what wise he might best make the place memorable, the green turf that covered so many noble warriors'.

Now Merlin, the Celtic magician who figures so prominently in the legends of Arthur, appears and makes a speech:

If thou be fain to grace the burial-place of these men with a work that shall endure for ever, send for the Dance of the Giants that is in Killaurus, a mountain in Ireland. For a structure of stones is there that none of his age could raise save his wit were strong enough to carry his art. For the stones be big, nor is there stone anywhere without virtue. And so they be set round this plot in a circle, even as they be now set up, here shall they stand for ever.

Geoffrey goes on:

The king burst out laughing and said, 'How may this be, that stones of such bigness and in a country so far away be brought hither, as if Britain were lacking in stones enough for the job?'

Merlin answered, 'Laugh not so lightly. In these stones is a mystery . . . and a healing virtue against many ailments. Giants of old did carry them from the furthest ends of Africa and did set them up in Ireland what time they did inhabit there. Not a stone is there that lacketh in virtue of witchcraft.'

Convinced, Ambrosius sent an expedition to fetch the stones. He was opposed by the Irish king, Gilloman, whom he quickly defeated. Transporting the stones, however, proved a more formidable task. Merlin watched the army using 'hawsers, ropes and scaling ladders' without success and he 'burst out laughing. He put together his own engines, laid the stones down so lightly as none would believe, and bade them carry them to the ships.'

They 'returned to Britain with joy and set them up about the compass of the burial-ground in such wise as they had stood upon mount Killaurus . . . and proved yet once again how skill surpasseth strength.'

The Merlin of Romance seems to have his origin with Geoffrey of Monmouth, and if, at some stage, there was confusion between the magician and the Devil, it could account for points of resemblance between Geoffrey of Monmouth's story and the one I heard from Wiltshire countrymen earlier this century. The period, of course, is entirely wrong. Stonehenge belongs to the centuries 1800 – 1400 BC, not to the time of the Saxon invasion. But the suggestion of the legendary value attached to the stones is interesting. And I am intrigued by the insistence that Merlin, the magician, transported the stones not by magic nor by tucking them under his arm and taking flight, but by specially-constructed 'engines', which conveyed them to the ships. In the Ministry of Works Guide Book Robert Newall explains that the blue stones probably did arrive from Wales, partly on sea and river transport by one of the various possible routes. This last detail, however, was soon lost, and when in the early years of the seventeenth-century Michael Drayton published his *Polyolbion,* he had returned to the version where Merlin brings the stones in a single night from Ireland to Wiltshire 'by his skill and magic's wondrous might'.

So we are left with the query, 'Which came first, the written tale as recounted by Geoffrey of Monmouth or the oral tradition current among local people earlier this century'? Did Geoffrey tap local sources in his day, or had someone who had read Geoffrey retold his story to people in the villages around Stonehenge? Or, as some suggest, did Geoffrey make it all up? Who can say?

I have never been able to find any evidence for the association of Druids with Stonehenge in local folklore. The idea was popularised by the Wiltshire antiquary, John Aubrey, who was born in 1627. After examining Stonehenge, Avebury and certain other monuments he wrote:

> I have, with humble submission to better judgments, offered a probability, that they were Temples of the Druids. My presumption is, That the Druids being the most eminent Priests, or Order of Priests, among the Britaines, 'tis odds but that these ancient monuments were Temples of the Priests of the most eminent Order, viz, Druids . . . This Inquiry, I must confess, is a gropeing in the Dark; but although I have not brought it into a clear light; yet I can affirm that I have brought it from utter darkeness to a thin mist, and have gone further in this Essay than any one before me.

The comment is appropriately diffident, but from it the Druid tradition subsequently grew. Aubrey was not, in fact, the first to suggest the association. Some fifty years earlier Inigo Jones, appointed by King James I to prepare a report on the stones, observed: 'Concerning the Druids, certainly Stonehenge could not be builded by them'. This negative conclusion shows that he had heard the theory. He is also right, since the Druids became established in Britain only about the third century BC. Robert Newall suggests, on the other hand, that being a comparatively knowledgeable class, they themselves possibly suggested their link with Stonehenge or even put it about that they built it.

Be that as it may, it was during the succeeding century that Druid fantasy flourished. Writer after writer took it up, embroidering it with snippets of circumstantial detail. One of the most enthusiastic was Dr William Stukeley, a celebrated antiquarian who describes Stonehenge as a serpent temple, and the Druids as priests. However, he did, make some original investigations in the neighbourhood and was perhaps the first to appreciate that the orientation of Stonehenge is towards the north-east, to the point at which the sun rises on Midsummer Day.

Even more fantastic was John Wood, who had much to do with the creation of eighteenth-century Bath and who established, to his own satisfaction, a connection between the Druids of Stonehenge, Pythagoras in Greece and Zoroaster in Persia. Since then increasingly wild theories, have assigned Stonehenge to the Phoenicians, the inhabitants of legendary Atlantis and, finally, to a tribe of North American Indians.

In 1781 'The Most Ancient Order of Druids' was founded in London. To this group belong the white-robed dignitaries who, when not disrupted by hooligans, assemble at Stonehenge for mystic rites at dawn on the Midsummer Solstice. By some these modern Druids are accepted as a genuine part of legendary Stonehenge, but there seems to be no valid evidence for any connection between their ritual and beliefs and those of the Druids of pre-Christian Britain.

The authentic Druids were an order of priests, magicians, medicine men or people of that nature who apparently established themselves in the Celtic lands of western Europe in the centuries following 500 BC. They were suppressed in Gaul by Julius Caesar and in Britain soon after the Roman conquest, though their influence lingered long afterwards. We have no real knowledge of their beliefs and activities; nearly all the meagre information at our disposal was filtered through hostile sources, such as Roman adversaries and monastic scribes. Some writers believe the Druids were a priesthood of advanced thinkers, possessed of much scientifice knowledge and motivated by a belief in one God. Others regard them as medicine-men who practised human sacrifice and even cannibalism. Perhaps the truth lies somewhere between these two extremes.

Stonehenge was built, in several stages, between 1800 and 1400 BC. Did the Druids on their arrival in Britain take over the thousand-year-old sacred site and use it for their own purposes, as missionaries of other new religions have done with sacred sites in many parts of the world? It is possible, but there is no evidence, one way or the other.

Avebury also tempted seventeenth-, eighteenth- and nineteenth-century antiquaries to effusions resembling those about Stonehenge, but with even more meagre evidence. There is little oral lore connected with the stone circle of Avebury. The chief local tradition concerns the technique for smashing the stones!

John Aubrey describes it in his *Natural History of Wiltshire:* 'They make a fire on that line of the stone where they would have it to crack; and, after the stone is well heated, draw over a line with cold water, and immediately give it a smart knock with a smyth's sledge, and it will break like the collets at the glass-house.'

John Britton, who edited and commented on the 1847 edition of Aubrey's work, remarks: 'This system of destruction is still adopted on the downs in the neighbourhood of Avebury. Many of the upright stones of the great Celtic temple in that parish have been thus destroyed in my time.'

Dr William Stukeley also gives a lively account of the operation, and a picture of the procedure is still extant.

Avebury is a much larger structure than Stonehenge, though not so elaborate. The stones are undressed and stand singly. Stonehenge is noted for its imposing trilithons, which are two massive upright stones supporting a third, as doorposts support a lintel. There are none at Avebury.

Avebury was apparently erected in two stages, between about 1700 and 1500 BC. The great circle, surrounded by ditches and banks, is spacious enough to hold the major part of the modern village of Avebury. Within it were once two smaller circles, and a third may have filled the space now occupied by the northern entrance. Around the inner edge of the encircling ditch were perched about a hundred huge stones, the heaviest of them weighing over 40 tons. Although not dressed, they seem to have been selected for their shape, stones with vertical sides, and others lozenge-shaped, standing alternately. They are typical of the sarsen stones found lying on the Marlborough Downs.

From a south-eastern point on the perimeter of Avebury circle a winding avenue marked by similar, though smaller, stones leads to the crest of Overton Hill, about two miles away. It is recorded that a stone circle stood here until early in the nineteenth century. Excavations in the 1930s revealed not only the holes in which the stones had stood but also several circles of holes for wooden posts. Archaeologists at present think that it may be older, by a few centuries, than the stone circle of Avebury.

Early antiquarians, like William Stukeley, fancied that the whole complex was a centre for serpent worship. Avebury itself, he thought, represented the coiled body of the serpent, its neck extended along Kennet avenue to the top of Overton Hill, the stone circle forming its head. A second winding avenue leading south-westwards to Beckhampton, where a few stones are standing, was supposed to be the serpent's tail. Modern authorities do not accept this explanation. However, 'The Sanctuary, a name given by the early investigators on Overton Hill, has been retained.

Just over a mile south of Avebury, between the river Kennet and the modern main road, is Silbury Hill. Guide books usually describe it as the largest artificial hill in Europe. Covering five acres and 130 feet high, it is made of chalk rubble from a nearby ditch. Once again, the Devil is said to have built Silbury, carrying the earth and chalk in a sack on his back, in a single night. According to another version, it is the burial mound of a king, named Sil, Seal or, in Wiltshire dialect, Zel. He was buried there erect, on horseback, and the whole task of raising the mound was completed 'while a posset of milk was seething'.

So there, somewhere in the depths of Silbury, should be the skeletons of the king and his horse, with his crown, his armour and his treasure. Excavations, begun in 1776, have been renewed at intervals since, and an elaborate operation, closely followed by television cameras, was mounted in 1969. Shafts have been sunk from top to bottom and bored in at the sides, but nothing of great importance has ever been discovered. However, according to local tradition, King Zel sometimes rides around the hill on moonlit nights, dressed in golden armour. A headless man is also said to have been seen.

In the eighteenth and early nineteenth centuries Palm Sunday was the occasion a procession of Avebury villagers to the top of Silbury 'to eat fig cakes and drink sugar and water' (see also p 53). Records describe the hill as crowded with people on Palm Sunday afternoons.

On one occasion during the First World War Miss Edith Olivier was surprised to see lights moving among the Avebury stones at night. She also heard gay music, of the kind associated with fairs, and assumed that one was being held there. Enquiries revealed that such a fair used to be held within the stone circle at Avebury though it been discontinued more than fifty years earlier. A teacher at Lackham School of Agriculture, passing Avebury one moonlit night not many years ago, was startled to see small figures moving among the stones.

In 1938 the skeleton of a man was found by excavators under one of the big stones of Avebury; it had evidently fallen on top of him. From the scissors he carried in his belt it seemed that he was a tailor; silver coins in his pouch dated his death at approximately 1320. It is assumed that he was helping with a stone-smashing operation when the boulder toppled over and crushed him, though there is no local tradition about him.

On the other side of the river Kennet is a spectacular prehistoric tomb, West Kennet Long Barrow. Probably built in about 2000 BC, which makes it earlier than Avebury and Stonehenge, it was evidently used as a kind of family vault for several centuries. Associated with it is the ghost of a man who is said to have been a priest. He has been seen entering the barrow at sunrise on the longest day, accompanied by a big white dog with red ears, the traditional fairy colouring.

Woodhenge, which can be termed a timber counterpart of Stonehenge and which stood about two miles north-east of it, was discovered by air photography in the 1920s. It stands just outside an enormous prehistoric circle of which virtually nothing is known. M. E. Cunnington, in her *Introduction to the Archaeology of Wiltshire,* records that one of the most striking features of Woodhenge was the burial 'in a grave occupying the same relative position to the rings that the 'altar' stone does to the circles of Stonehenge. The burial was that of a young child, about three years of age, whose skull had been cleft before burial, thus suggesting that the burial was in the nature of a dedicatory or sacrificial one.'

The Wiltshire downs, and particularly Salisbury Plain, contain one of the largest concentrations of barrows in Europe. In some of those which have been excavated, treasure has been found – objects of gold, copper, bronze and amber. Although a number of these barrows were opened by local people, before archaeologists became interested in them, few legends attached to them. But they were sometimes linked with the Devil, as in The Devil's Den, or with giants, as in The Giant's Grave. The Devil's Den, a megalithic grave near Marlborough, is haunted by a dog, with huge, burning eyes. It is white and apparently has its kennel underneath the tomb. Sometimes at night the Devil can be seen trying to shift the stones with the help of four white oxen. Doghill Barrow, near Stonehenge, also has a ghostly dog.

A barrow on Roundway Down, near Devizes, was haunted by a human ghost, which led people to it, though since 1855, when the barrow was excavated, the ghost has not been seen.

Manton barrow, near Marlborough, which was excavated in 1906, contained the body of an old woman adorned with ornaments of gold, amber, bronze and lignite. Nearby was a cottage occupied by a widow whose husband had been employed by a Dr J. B. Maurice of Marlborough. After the excavation and the reinterment of the skeleton, the barrow was made up and planted with trees. The widow told Dr Maurice that 'every night since that man from Devizes came and disturbed 'the old creature' she did come out of the mound and walk around the house and squinny into the window. I do hear her most nights and want you to give me summat to keep her away.' The doctor gave her some medicine, telling her to go to bed in the dark immediately after taking it. Later the widow said. 'The old creature came round the cottage as usual for a few nights but, not seeing me, gave up, thinking, no doubt, she had scared me away.'

2 The Hill Fairs

WINDMILL HILL, near Avebury, is a rounded chalk hill, typical of so many in Wiltshire. The contours around its summit are etched with three concentric lines of earthworks, partly destroyed by ploughing. The site was excavated in the 1920s and yielded much information about the life and culture of the neolithic people who lived there from about 2400 BC, According to the official guide-book: 'The earthwork enclosure ... seems to have been used as a cattle pound, in which the herds were rounded up in the autumn. The gaps in the ditches cannot all have been entrances, and are probably the result of splitting up the work of digging among several gangs. The banks inside the ditches may have been topped with continuous fences or hedges of thorn.

No trace of houses of any permanent settlement was found inside the earthworks; but in the ditches, and especially the outer one, the excavators found numerous camp-fires, broken pottery and animals' bones, which suggest that parties of herdsmen used the shelter of the ditches to camp out for a few days each year while the cattle were being rounded up.'

Wiltshire has an abundance of hill forts, which are hill-tops fortified by a ditch and earthen rampart, or by a series of concentric ditches and banks. Many of them are elaborately designed and very strong. The fortifications in most instances date from the Iron Age – say, a century or two BC. There is a suggestion that some at least may have been constructed in the face of a challenge by the invading Belgae, who had already established themselves in south-eastern Britain.

However, the complex system of fortifications that many of them now exhibit is a late addition. In Windmill Hill we see the earliest protoype – a simple cattle corral. Several of the simpler hill-top earthworks in Wiltshire likewise show little or no evidence of permanent human occupation. Figsbury Ring, near Salisbury, is a notable example. Others are Knook Down and Cold Berwick Down. So we can imagine the hill-top corrals being used for the seasonal gatherings of flocks and herds from their pastures on the rolling downs. These assemblies would be for branding and shearing, for the dispersal and slaughter of stock, and perhaps for communal lambing behind a rampart against wolves and bears.

There are two natural calendars of some antiquity in Britain. One is the agricultural calendar, with Quarter Days on Lady Day, Midsummer Day, Michaelmas and Christmas. The other is pastoral and Celtic, with Quarter Days on February 1st, May 1st, August 1st and November 1st. This one is much older and dates from the time before extensive cultivation of crops.

We know the Celtic names for the Quarter Days, or prime festivals. February 1st was Imbolc, later identified with Candlemas and coinciding with the beginning of lambing. May 1st is Beltane, which marks the return of summer; probably on this date the new crop of lambs and calves were branded and turned out to graze. August 1st was Lugnasad. This seems to have been borrowed from the agricultural calendar, for it is the festival of the first-fruits, marking the beginning of harvest, which in later times was known as Lammas. However, the date may have had an earlier pastoral significance which escapes us. November 1st was Samhain, when the flocks and herds were rounded up after their summer on the open downs. The surplus animals were slaughtered, and sheep were mated for next season's lamb crop. Samhain in due course became All Saints' Day. October 31st, the eve of Samhain, thus became Hallowe'en, when witches and devils were active on the earth.

The feast days were naturally marked by a gathering of the clans, with eating, drinking and revelry. The obvious meeting-place would be the livestock corrals. The tradition seems to have lingered longest in connection with the autumn round-up. Until the outbreak of the First World War autumn fairs were held on at least three hill-top sites in Wiltshire. These were Yarnbury Castle, on the downs above Wylye, Westbury Hill and Cold Berwick Hill, near Fonthill. They were primarily sheep fairs, but some cattle, horses and dogs were sold and there were usually a number of cheapjacks and gipsies about.

One reason why the hill-top fairs survived to such a late date is that they served a useful purpose. They were convenient centres for the great sheep farms which occupied most of the downland. Nevertheless, the sites were bleak and exposed, and the sheep farmers liked attending valley fairs, as at Wilton and Britford. The hill-top sites represented an ancient tradition. One of the fairs, Yarnbury Castle, was actually held within the ramparts of an old hill fort. Westbury Hill Fair was sited on the windy crest just above the figure of the White Horse, but it may have been moved, at some time, from the earthwork known as Bratton Castle, a mile or so along the hill. Cold Berwick Hill has no earthwork but is near one of the most extensive areas of ancient downland settlement in the county.

It may well be that many of the older early sheep fairs had similar origins, even if they did not occupy hill-top sites. The hill-top earthworks probably survived largely because, after the coming of the Saxons, people preferred to live in the valleys. Any valley earthworks were therefore likely to be demolished, to make room for new buildings, yet the tradition surrounding them could have remained.

This could well be true of Marlborough. One of its most outstanding features is an extraordinarily broad High Street – so broad that nowadays there is room for a car park along the centre with a free flow of traffic on either side. The space occupied by the car park was once used for sheep pens. Here enormous numbers of sheep were sold at Marlborough Fair, known throughout southern England, or rather, Fairs, for in the nineteenth century there were three at Marlborough, one on 11 July, one on 22 August and one on 23 November. There were also two hiring fairs 'one on the Saturday before Old Michaelmas and one after'. All were accompanied by the usual ancillary activities. The folk of Marlborough naturally used their broad High Street for celebrating. Sir Richard Colt Hoare, the Wiltshire antiquary and historian of the early nineteenth century, records, for instance, a visit to Marlborough on some festival day when he found '1333 partakers of conviviality seated at one long table from the market house to St Peter's Church, nearly half-a-mile'. Let us hope that it kept fine.

Here we have, almost certainly, an example of a town growing up around a sheep fair site, and that, a long time ago. The very name is suggestive. Etymologists of the nineteenth century, note that Marlborough derives from 'the marle [or chalk] borough', or possibly from 'maer borough' – the borough on the boundary. But more recent writers incline to a different view. The authors of *The Place Names of Wiltshire*, published in 1939, say that it probably means 'the barrow of one Maerla', assuming this to be an obscure Old English name. 'There can be little doubt', they add, 'that the *beorg* has reference to the artificial mound of very ancient date which formed the nucleus of the Castle. *Maerla* may have been its sometime owner or the name of someone who had been buried there.'

The mound in question is like a miniature Silbury. Unlike Silbury and many other Wiltshire prehistoric sites, however, it has found itself in the centre of much subsequent development. In Norman times it was incorporated into a castle, and now stands in the grounds of Marlborough College. Local tradition has no doubt about its significance. Marlborough's motto is *Tibi nunc sapientis ossa Merlini?* – 'Where now are the bones of wise Merlin?' Answer: 'Under the mound at Marlborough'. Marlborough, then is 'Merlins barrow', and, if we are to follow this attractive line of argument, Marlborough's fair may be seen as a link with tribal assemblies, combining religious, commercial and social functions, once held around the magic mound of Merlin. Against this, unfortunately, must be argued the fact that Marlborough's name, in virtually its present form, was well established before Geoffrey of Monmouth popularised Merlin in England. In doing so he not only drew on Welsh tradition but borrowed, using his own phonetics, the name of a Welsh diviner, Myrddin. *The Place-Names of Wiltshire* suggests Maerla as cognate with the Germanic Merila.

3   Hill Carvings

GEORGE STUBBS, the eighteenth-century painter of horses and other animal subjects, may have a further claim to distinction. It seems that he may have been indirectly responsible for the rash of white horses adorning the chalk hills of Wiltshire. It was an age of follies and other examples of ostentatious landscaping, and once one white horse had been carved in hillside chalk others soon followed.

It was in 1776 that Stubbs, visiting Brocklesby Park in Lincolnshire, began the series of portraits of horses, hounds and huntsmen which made him the most popular painter of his day. Among his friends and admirers was a Dr Christopher Alsop, of Calne. In 1780 he set about carving a white horse on a convenient hillside in the neighbouring parish of Cherhill. There can be little doubt that the Cherhill Horse was inspired by the rather plump, stocky horses with docked tails which Stubbs loved to paint.

Wiltshire has eleven white horses, far more than any other

county. Most of them seem to belong to the late eighteenth or early nineteenth centuries.

The Alton Barnes Horse, about five miles from the Cherhill example, is said to have been cut in 1812 by a travelling artist who was paid £20 for his work by a local farmer, Mr. Robert Pile. Although on a gentler slope than most white horses, it is visible from long distances.

The Hackpen Horse is on the north-western scarp of the Marlborough Downs, on the slopes of towering Hackpen Hill, near the village of Broad Hinton. It is not a large horse and not well sited, on a slope of only 30 degrees. It is said to have been cut by the parish clerk of Broad Hinton to celebrate the coronation of Queen Victoria in 1838.

The Marlborough Horse is even smaller but can be seen, by those who know where to look, from the Bath road, south-east of Marlborough. The boys of a school at Marlborough – not Marlborough College cut it in 1804. After falling into disrepair it was restored in 1873.

In the Pewsey Vale, the Pewsey Horse is even more recent, having been cut to commemorate the coronation of King George VI in 1937. The artist was Mr. George Marples, an expert on hillside figures. His son, Mr. Morris Marples, reproduces in his ˙book *White Horses and Other Hill Figures* (1949) the working plan used. It employs an ingenious system of triangulation, worked out by Mr. Marples himself.

On the same hill, lower down and a little to the right, was an older Pewsey Horse. This was cut in the eighteenth century by the same Robert Pile who paid for the Alton Barnes figure.

On a hill to the north-east of the village of Broadtown, facing Wootton Bassett, is a rather small horse. It is said to have been originally cut by a local farmer, Mr William Simmonds, in the 1860s.

Three other horses have almost completely disappeared. One was the Inkpen Horse, on the slopes of Ham Hill, where the counties of Hampshire, Wiltshire and Berkshire meet. It was cut by a local landowner, a Mr Wright, in the 1860s. The second was the Devizes Horse, on Roundway Hill, just north of the town. The shoemakers of Devizes were said to have carved it at a Whitsuntide festival in 1845. In 1949 traces of a hitherto unknown horse were discovered on Rockley Down, a few miles north-east of Marlborough. Nothing is known of its history, but it resembles the eighteenth- and nineteenth-century figures.

We have left till last the biggest and best-known white horse, that at Westbury. Before looking at it more closely, let us briefly note some of Wiltshire's other hill figures. Travellers along the A30 road west of Salisbury will see a collection of regimental badges and an outline map of Australia on Fovant Down. These were cut by soldiers camping under the hill in the First World War. Another figure of the same period is the Bulford Kiwi, carved by New Zealand troops in 1918. Most recent of all is the head of a panda which appeared overnight in the late 1960s on a hillside about two miles east of Salisbury and overlooking the main London-Salisbury road. It was cut by students, who must have worked hard to complete it in one night – and in the dark, too.

Now let us turn to the majestic White Horse that looks westwards from the slopes of Westbury Hill across the lovely meadows of Blackmore Vale. Tradition is inclined to give it an early date; a favourite tale is that it was carved to commemorate Alfred's victory over the Danes in 878. (This, naturally, presupposes that the site of the Battle of Ethandune was on this hilltop.)

However the first mention of the Horse in literature, is in the writings of Rev. F. Wise, Keeper of the Radcliffe Library in Oxford, who stated in 1742 that the figure had been 'wrought within the memory of persons now living or but lately dead'. The carving of the present Horse in 1778 is recorded. It is said to have replaced an earlier one, presumably the figure mentioned by Wise. The date would make even the 1778 Westbury Horse the earliest in Wiltshire by two years, and its realistic lines suggest Stubbs' influence.

A surviving drawing of the older Westbury Horse shows such a completely different animal as to throw doubt on Wise's statement that it was cut within the memory of people living in 1742. The figure had a long drooping body, very short legs and goggle eyes. On the tip of its tail was poised a crescent moon, horns upwards. Like the Uffington Horse in Berkshire and unlike the present Westbury Horse, it faced right. Most authorities think that it was absorbed in the body of the present Horse in 1778.

If Wise was mistaken in the modest age he gives to the older Westbury Horse, the error could perhaps have come about through confusion between original carving and scouring.

Every so often, hillside figures need to be scoured, to clear away the creeping turf, and it is likely that many such carvings have been lost through neglect in cleaning them. Tradition says that White Horses should be scoured once every seven years, but few attained the ideal. Records show that scourings of the Uffington Horse (Berkshire) took place in 1755, 1776, 1780, 1785, 1803, 1808, 1813, 1825, 1838, 1843 and 1857. The intervals are thus anything from four to twenty-one years.

Carving or scouring a Horse is generally a community affair. Mr Pile's travelling artist was the exception. More usual were the boys of Marlborough School, the shoemakers of Devizes, and the soldiers of Salisbury Plain. Associating a periodic scouring with a fete, fair or some other celebration would seem an obvious means of getting a group of workers for the job.

Scourings of the Uffington White Horse were traditionally occasions for festivities. It is said that more than 30,000 people attended the scouring there on Whit-Monday, 1780. A novelist, Thomas Hughes, even wrote a book about it, *The Scouring of the White Horse,* published in 1889, to which we are indebted for much information about what went on at these celebrations.

It seems that the scourings of Wiltshire horses were also an excuse for celebrating. Rev. F. Wise mentions, in 1742, that the inhabitants of Westbury used to meet for a 'revel or festival' on Westbury White Horse. Morris Marples, accepting Wise's statement that the first Westbury Horse had been carved not more than fifty or sixty years before that date, suggests that the Horse was a deliberate copy of the Uffington example and that the 'revels' may have been a deliberate imitation of the Uffington 'pastime'. That may be so, but it is just possible that Wise's informants were confusing a scouring with a cutting and that the Horse may be very much older. The illustration given of it in Gough's edition of Camden's *Britannica* does indeed look stylised rather than an attempt to depict real horse-flesh. There is a suggestion, too, that the Cherhill Horse as it now appears was preceded by an older carving, but the theory depends on some doubtful mediaeval references.

When they were investigating the White Horses Mr Morris Marples and his father came across several apparently contradictory statements about dates. For instance, the

Broadtown White Horse is stated by Rev. W. C. Plenderleath – Rector of Cherhill who published several monographs on white horses between 1870 and 1885 – to have been cut in 1864. However, a distinguished contributor, a curator of the Imperial War Museum, said in 1919 that he remembered helping to *scour* this Horse when a boy at school at Wootton Bassett in 1863. Another informant told Mr George Marples in about 1936 that this same Horse had been cut about forty years earlier by a Mr Horsey, who lived locally. Two out of the three must be wrong. One feels tempted to accept the earliest dates and to assume that the other chroniclers were mistaken, or were at least confusing a scouring with a cutting. All that can be said is that some of the Wiltshire White Horses may be conceivably older than the eighteenth- or nineteenth-century dates they are usually assigned but how much older is impossible to say.

Morris Marples records, of the older Pewsey Horse: 'After 1789 the scouring was discontinued, because the owner of the land objected to the festivities which accompanied it.'

The Marlborough Horse was scoured regularly by the boys of the school which first carved it. Says Mr Marples: 'We are told that the ceremony was one of the most cherished traditions of the school. One can well imagine that it called for a holiday and appropriate celebrations'. The school was closed down in 1830.

Nowadays it is possible to give the hillside White Horses a permanent facing, using a form of concrete. In the early 1950s Messrs Chivers of Devizes were employed to give this treatment to the Uffington Horse, and I accompanied the head of the firm to see the work in progress. His foreman had discovered that, if he stood at a certain point on the shoulder of the hill opposite the White Horse, he could give instructions in a normal, almost whispered voice to men at work on the figure, a quarter to half a mile away; the hill was a gigantic whispering gallery.

4 Festivals of May and Whitsun

'FRIENDS! there's a good echo here! Let it ring!' The score or so people, assembled before the high altar of Salisbury Cathedral but quite unabashed by their surroundings, took the cue from their leader. Obediently they gave their traditional cry: 'Grovely! Grovely! Grovely! and all Grovely!'

They had just presented their offering of green boughs to the Dean, before the altar. Now, they filed out by way of the great west door and gathered on the daisy-sprinkled lawn. There half-a-dozen or so of them, dressed in early Victorian costume, danced the traditional measure, before climbing aboard a motor-coach for the return journey to Wishford, eight miles away up the Wylye valley.

The crowd assembled to watch the ceremony when last I was there, a few years ago, was remarkably small, no doubt because this annual occasion is not widely known. The Wishford Oak Apple celebrations, of which this is a part, are not organised with an eye to publicity, though the public are welcome to attend if they happen to hear about it. What goes on at Wishford is artless and spontaneous participation in an age-old celebration for its own sake. Whether there are spectators or not matters not at all to the villagers.

On Oak Apple Day, 29 May, the sun rises at 4.50 a.m. and the lark gets up half-an-hour earlier, but anyone who wants to start the day with Wishford has to do better than that. One year when I was to have the honour of making the speech at the lunch later in the day I determined to be in at the very beginning. So I arrived in the village at 3.30 a.m., only to find the earliest performers preparing to go home.

These were the members of the tin-pan band which from half-past-two onwards had been forcing the villagers out of bed. Each house received a visit and was not left in peace until the householder came to the door to prove that he was awake – although he might not look it! – and was preparing to take part. Instruments of the 'band' were coal-shovels, dust-bin lids, drums, recorders and anything else which would make a noise. It was interesting to see that the 'musicians' were not elderly villagers consciously preserving a tradition but local youngsters, mostly teenagers, both boys and girls, in jeans and leather jerkins. No doubt it was a delight to them to be able to make such a hullaballoo with the approval of their elders.

In the first dawn twilight the villagers began to leave their homes and follow the ancient sunken way between cultivated fields to the Forest of Grovely, which is thrown like a blanket over the crest of the ridge between the Wylye and Nadder valleys. As, just before five, I stood on the edge of the wood and watched the sun float up from the rim of Salisbury Plain, some were already tramping back down again, bearing their trophies. Most had green boughs cut from the oak-trees to decorate their houses, but I was pleased to see that a number of practical gardeners had cut bundles of hazel rods for their summer's supply of beansticks.

Accompanied by my host, the Rector of Wishford, I penetrated farther into the oakwoods in search of oak-apples. A prize is offered to the bearer of the branch with the greatest number of those large, soft, blush-tinted galls – the work, incidentally, of a tiny gallfly *Biorrhiza terminalis*. Another prize goes to the house most attractively decorated with green oak boughs, but we could not participate in this, for one cannot do everything, and we were too busy dragging back a huge oak bough which we proposed to hoist to the top of St Giles' church tower. And so we did, with the aid of a dozen muscular men and several pulleys. There it hung, a slash of greenery against the grey stone, the red cross of St George billowing above it, while we went home to breakfast.

No organiser of a tourist attraction would have permitted the two-hour time-lap which now occurred. The villagers disappeared, and nothing happened till after ten o'clock, when the bus came to take the delegation to Salisbury Cathedral. On their return lunch in Wishford was attended by local dignitaries, including the mayors of Salisbury and Wilton, after which the celebrations followed the usual lines of a village fête.

Ostensibly Wishford Oak Apple Day commemorates the villagers' victory, two centuries or so ago, over an Earl of Pembroke, the local landowner, who tried to interfere with their immemorial rights to gather green branches in Grovely Forest. But documentary evidence confirms that the celebrations are much older than that.

The Sum of the Ancient Customs belonging to Wishford and Barford out of the Forest of Grovely is the title of a document prepared in the reign of Henry VIII, at the time of the dissolution of monasteries. Besides confirming that the villagers may gather wood in the Forest, send cattle and pigs to graze there and kill one fat buck every Whitsuntide, the deed testifies to the antiquity, even at that date, of some of the associated customs.

> The Lords, Freeholders, Tenants and Inhabitants of the Manor of Great Wishford, or so many of them as would, in ancient time, have used to go in a dance to the Cathedral Church of Our Blessed Lady in the city of New Sarum on Whit Tuesday, in the said county of Wilts, and there they made their claim to the custom in the forest of Grovely in these words: 'Grovely! Grovely! Grovely! and all Grovely!'

There were other features of the celebrations, now discontinued. The fat buck, mentioned above, was to be provided by the forest ranger of Grovely, who had to deliver one half of the animal to Wishford and one half to Barford, for the village feast. If he failed, the villagers had the right to go into the forest and kill one. If, on the other hand, he complied with the custom, he was to receive from each of the manors 'one white Loaf and one Gallon of Beer and A Pair of Gloves or twelve pence in money'.

On their excursion to Salisbury Cathedral the villagers had to pay their 'pentecostals' or 'smoke farthings'. Until some time in the nineteenth century the dancing on the Cathedral green was accompanied by a kind of fair, with stalls and sideshows, very like a modern village fete. This was discontinued, and the dancing is a fairly recent revival.

The forest rights claimed in the Tudor document are typical of the rights once claimed by most English villages over the waste land beyond the enclosed fields. There the common people supplemented the income from their small farms by gathering dead wood, cutting turf for fuel, pasturing cattle, gathering nuts and acorns and allowing pigs to root. It is said that the inhabitants of Barford St Martin, on the other side of Grovely Wood, forfeited their rights long ago by accepting a commutation into an annual payment of sacks of coal for the village poor – a type of encroachment common enough when waste land was reclaimed for cultivation or enclosed by game-preserving landowners. The people of Wishford, for their part, resolved that their determination to stick to their rights should be clearly understood, hence the insistence on the old ritual.

Although the present Wishford celebrations are held on Oak Apple Day, 29 May, the Tudor document states that they occurred on Whit Tuesday. So it could be that we are dealing with festivities transferred from May Day.

Amesbury, a few miles away had its own May Day feast, at which the May Queen danced for the Chimney Sweep. It was known as the Sweep's Holiday, which suggests that the Sweep was the main character. The custom died out within the memory of people still alive in the 1930s.

On Old May Day a fair and festivities were held at the Cross Stones near Durrington, near the spot where Woodhenge was subsequently discovered. In *Moonrakings*, a collection of Wiltshire stories complied by Miss Edith Olivier the day's events are described:

First of all, the men went to the downs and got a may bush and then to the Nag's Head Inn for the May-pole. They tied the bush to the top of the May-pole and chained the pole to the top of the Cross Stones. All this happened the night before, when it was dark.

In the evening of Old May Day they danced around the Cross Stones to the music of concertinas and whistle-pipes. They also had cakes and barrels of beer to eat and drink.

Mere had a fair on 17 May, when there was folk dancing in the market place. This was probably the occasion referred to in a survey of 1602, though the document calls the event the 'Whitsuntide church ales'. It states that at Whitsuntide

> the neighbours meet at the church-house, and there meetly feed on their owne victuals, contributing some petty portion to the stock which by many smalls groweth to a meetly greatness; for there is entertayned a kinde of emulation betweene these wardens, who by his graciousness in gathering and good husbandry can best advance the churches profit. Besides the neighbour parishes at those times lovingly visit one another and this way frankely spend their money together. The afternoones are consumed in such exercises as olde and yonge folke (having leysure) doe accustomally weare out the time withall.

Some scholars consider that, at least in the sixteenth century, Mere had Church Ales at Easter, and that it was connected with the 'Cuckowe King'. The Church-Wardens' accounts for Mere begin in 1556, but there is no reference to any 'Cuckowe King' for the first nine years. Then in 1565, he is recorded, with the added detail he was Prynce in the preceding year, 'according to Custome'. Evidently it was the rule that the man appointed 'Prynce' one year became 'Cuckowe King' in the next, though in 1566 provision was made for a substitute king if the incumbent, who had been unwell, could not 'serve at the tyme of the Church Ale'.

Swindon had a fair on the second Monday after 12 May, while Newnton, in north Wiltshire, observed some interesting customs on Trinity Sunday, described by John Aubrey, the seventeenth century antiquary:

Upon every Trinity Sunday, the Parishioners being come to the door of the Hayward's House, the door was struck thrice, in honour of the Holy Trinity; then they entered. The Bell was rung; after which, silence being ordered, they read their prayers aforesaid.

Then was a Ghirland of Flowers (about the year 1660 one was killed trying to take away the Ghirland) made upon a Hoop, brought forth by a Maid of the Town upon her Neck, and a Young Man (a Bachelor) of another Parish, first saluted her three times, in honour of the Trinity, in respect of God the Father. Then she puts the Ghirland upon his neck, and kisses him three times, in honour of the Trinity, particularly God the Son. Then he puts the Ghirland on her neck again, and kisses her three times, in respect of the Holy Trinity, and particularly the Holy Ghost. Then he takes the Ghirland from her neck, and, by the Custom, must give her a penny at least, which, as Fancy leads, is now exceeded, as 2s. 6d &c. The method of giving this Ghirland is from House to House annually, till it comes round.

In the evening every Commoner sends his supper up to this House, which is called the Eale House; and having before laid in there equally a Stock of Malt, which was brewed in the House, they sup together, and what was left was given to the poor.

The exaggerated insistence that this was a Christian festival, honouring the Trinity, suggests that in its origin it was probably nothing of the kind!

J. P. Emslie sent a note to Folk-Lore in 1900, describing May garlanding at Wilton and Salisbury on May Day, 1896. At Wilton things evidently started early, for by 9 a.m. the little girls who had taken part were 'wandering aimlessly about with their garlands or sitting on doorsteps counting their gains'. The garlands, or sometimes simply bunches of flowers, were mounted on little sticks, and the girls went from house to house in groups singing a song the final line of which was 'Please give a penny for the garland'. Emslie adds that 'Wilton is a small town, and the garlands were numerous . . . ' The money was collected so that the girls could enjoy themselves at Wilton Fair, held on the first Monday in May.

He then went to Salisbury, where garlanding was still in

progress at 11 o'clock. The custom was quite different, as the girls went about in pairs with their garland strung from a short stick, which they held between them. The garlands themselves were very elaborate – crowns, with the circlet and bows covered in flowers. Apparently the tour, the object of which was also to collect pennies, was confined largely to the shops, and Emslie heard no singing.

Miss Olivier has collected the reminiscences of a Women's Institute member at Woodford, a village close to Stonehenge.

My earliest recollections were May-day Festivals. Leaving my home at Heale Park, we gathered at the School with our garlands. From there we made our way through the village, singing out May Songs at the different houses on the way, our last call being at Mrs Elizabeth Pile, at Upper Woodford. Then we made our way up Barlin Hill to Druids' Lodge, which was inhabited by Mrs Wilcot. We always had a hearty welcome there, coming away richer by five shillings, which was a large sum in those days. Coming home over the downs we had rare good fun, reaching School in time for tea, which was thoroughly enjoyed.

Much the same distance from Stonehenge, about three miles, is Berwick St James, which had a Village Club with a Whitsuntide feast. Miss Edith Olivier has again given us the recollections of a local resident:

On Monday the members of the Club did form up in double line at the Boot Inn; the village brass band did go to Crisscross to meet the Vicar and his two daughters, and march to the Boot Inn in front of the band. Then the members did fall in behind the band with their Club sticks, which were painted red, white and blue, wearing top hats with rosettes and streamers flying, marching through village to the church, where a service was held. After the service the procession marched back to the Boot Inn, where dinner was prepared by the stewards of the Club in the old Barn. The chair was taken by the Vicar. After dinner the Club members, with their band, did march to Winterbourne Stoke to the Vicarage, where dancing was indulged in on the lawn for an hour; then, returning to the

village, visited the principal houses, when again dancing
was indulged in for the evening . . .

Edith Olivier's informant told her that this custom came to
an end in 1874, but it must have experienced a revival some
twenty years or so later. At that time, not having a band of its
own, Berwick used to hire one from another village. It would
have been about the year 1900 when Pitton Band, with my
father as bandmaster, did the honours. My father used to say
he remembered only too well that long march from Berwick to
Winterbourne Stoke and back again!

The Village Club was a feature of most Wiltshire villages in
the nineteenth century. Ostensibly it was a primitive
insurance society. Members paid their dues weekly and were
entitled to sick pay when ill. Many, perhaps most, of the
Clubs were 'slate clubs'. The accounts were kept on a slate,
usually at the village inn, and were wiped off at the end of the
year. Any balance remaining at that date was used to treat all
the members.

The Club year usually ended at Whitsuntide, probably a
coincidence, for so many villages had preserved a tradition of
Whitsuntide feasts, 'ales' or revels that it was natural for the
Clubs to adopt an existing festival rather than start up a new
one. The Clubs thus inherited, continued or modified many
old customs.

There was a further twist to the long story. During the
second half of the nineteenth century the total abstinence
movement became strong in the villages and many Bands of
Hope were founded. The Whitsuntide Club feasts were
notorious for the tendency of members to become drunk. In a
counter-attack, therefore, the temperance advocates, from
their strongholds in the village chapels, settled on Whitsuntide
for Sunday School anniversaries. Whitsuntide became the
children's festival – an occasion for song, recitations and, on
Whit Monday, a public tea, with races, sweet scrambles and
other respectable attractions.

In the end, respectability won, largely because the village
clubs disappeared with the introduction of a national
insurance scheme. The Sunday Schools were left masters in
a now uncontested field. In my native village of Pitton their
triumph was complete; for in 1888 the Methodists erected
their new village chapel in a corner of Club Close, where the

revels had traditionally been held, and took over Club Close itself for their Whitsuntide celebrations. Now, of course, Whitsuntide has surrendered much of its significance to the new Spring Festival decreed by the Government, and such Sunday School anniversaries as survive seem to have lost their roots in the calendar.

In a little book on Everley, published in 1967, Mr. W. A. Edwards recalls the Everley Club festival.

Whit Monday was the day when the annual feast was held, and this was the one occasion of the year when members of the family who had migrated to town or elsewhere always tried to visit the old home. All members paraded and marched to Church for morning service behind a brass band, each man wearing rosettes of red, white and blue and carrying painted staves with fluttering ribbons. At the head of the procession walked the Secretary wearing a broad blue sash, and on each side of him were carried the Club standards ... Penalty for failing to attend Church was a fine of 2/6, and for failing to follow the Club afterwards in its perambulations around the village a fine of 1/- was imposed. A substantial dinner was provided at the Crown Inn, and afterwards visits were paid to the principal residents, and a programme of music given.

This Club provided sick pay for fourteen weeks at 8s 6d per week, and thereafter 4s 3d per week for apparently an unlimited period. It does not, however, seem to have been a slate club.

Another village club that was not a slate club was the Besom Club at Harnham. Its official name was the Harnham Friendly Society but it was called the Besom Club because when it went on parade on Whit Mondays its members carried besoms as well as banners and staves. Subscriptions were a shilling a year. Sick members received an allowance according to their needs, and if a member or his wife died every member had to pay a shilling towards the funeral expenses. The Whit Monday celebrations started, as usual, with a church service. Then the Club paraded the village, led by Odstock brass band. They went to the Swan Inn for dinner and visited two other inns during the day. In the evening they finished up with dancing in a field.

The *History of Harnham,* compiled in 1952-54 by the Harnham Women's Institute, records that:

> the Rev. C. D. Crawley, who was Vicar from 1881 to 1888, did not altogether approve of so much drinking and hilarity for the children of the parish, so he used to borrow a big farm waggon from Mr. Bowns, pack all the children in it, and take them up to the Race Plain for a picnic, and games. But alas, as soon as he brought them home, they raced up to the field to join in that fun, too!

The village Club at Landford was known as The Foresters' Club. The 'fair' which it held on the Thursday after Whitsun seems to have followed the usual pattern of village festivities. There were sundry stalls and competitions, and a dinner for all club members was provided at Manor Farm. Says the Landford Women's Institute in its Scrap Book for the parish: 'The Band of Hope made great efforts to keep the young people from attending it.'

One of the earliest references to a village club, or rather, its predecessor, is in the writings of John Aubrey. Referring to his own village, Kington St. Michael, he writes:

> There were no rates for the poor in my Grandfather's days; for Kingstone St Michael the Church Ale at Whitsuntide did the business. In every parish is (or was) a church house, to which belonged spits, crocks, etc, utensils for dressing provisions. Here the housekeepers met and were merry, and gave their charity. The young people were there, too, and had dancing, bowling, shooting at butts, etc., the ancients sitting gravely by, and looking on. All things were civil, and without scandal.

From this it appears that church ales were recognised as media for charity before village clubs were in existence to organise Whitsuntide feasts.

Aubrey was writing of the days before the Puritan Commonwealth, when maypoles were erected in nearly every village in England. The Puritans, not agreeing that such activities were 'without scandal', thoroughly disapproved of them. Wrote one: 'If Moses were angry when he saw the people dance about a golden calf, well may we be angry to see people dancing the morrice about a pole in honour of a whore . . .

After the Restoration, in 1660, it became permissible to erect maypoles again. Many villages did not revive the old customs, though in Wiltshire, Ansty still has a pole 70 feet high and maintains the celebrations in traditional style.

Downton Spring Fair, once held on 23 April but long since discontinued, may seem early in the year for May Day associations, but one aspect is reminiscent of Mere's 'Cuckowe King'. (see page 40) For villages north of Downton, 23 April was traditionally the date when 'they opened the gate at Downton to let the Cuckoo through'. Another version, unflattering to the people of Downton, states that the villagers shut the Cuckoo in Downton pound and were startled when it flew out, over the top of the rails.

The hobby-horse is a character in the May Day plays, and Salisbury has a splendid example in its Hob-nob, which is housed in Salisbury Museum. With the Salisbury Giant, it is brought on special occasions – pageants, coronations and carnivals (see pp 111-112).

Mediaeval sources which mention 'Riding the Jorge' at Salisbury may refer to the Hob-nob. It has been suggested, too, that originally the procession may have taken place on St George's Day (23 April) and not as in later years on 24 June, the patronal festival of the Tailors' Guild.

Charlton, in the Vale of Pewsey, has a feast with a strange background, which seems at first to have nothing to do with May-Day or early summer festivals, although it is held on 1 June. This is the 'Duck Feast', ostensibly in memory of Stephen Duck, the eighteenth century labourer poet.

Stephen Duck was born at Charlton in 1705 and for most of his early manhood worked as a casual labourer on farms in the neighbourhood. In particular he was an expert thresher, and one of his best poems, most of which are no more than mediocre, is *The Thresher's Labour*. His verses attracted the attention of local gentry, one of whom introduced him at Court in London, where he became a nine days' wonder. Queen Caroline took an interest in him, paid him a pension and appointed him Keeper of her library. When, however, the novelty wore off, Stephen found himself ignored by courtiers and rival poets, who continually reminded him of his social inferiority. Eventually he committed suicide by drowning.

The annual feast in his memory is held at the Charlton Cat inn. Known as the Duck Feast, it is attended by thirteen Duck Men, one of whom, the president, is the Chief Duck. He wears a tall hat trimmed with duck feathers and bearing the figure of a thresher with his flails. Toasts are drunk from The Duck Goblet, including one to Lord Palmerston who in 1734 gave a piece of land, the rent of which was to pay for the feast.

It is worth noting that in 1734 Stephen Duck was only twenty-nine years old. He lived until 1756. One does not normally institute a commemorative feast for a living man, particularly one with the best part of his career still in front of him. Perhaps this Duck Feast has something in common with the Aldbourne Feast, which features a dabchick.

The story of the Aldbourne dabchick is as follows.

Long ago, on the little pond in the middle of Aldbourne village a dabchick was found. None of the villagers had ever seen such a bird before, which is not surprising, for Aldbourne is a downland village unlikely to attract a dabchick. They sent for the oldest inhabitant, an ancient invalid who had to be fetched in a wheelbarrow (cf. the Ticktoad at All Cannings, p. 180). After he had been wheeled round the pond three times he declared that the bird was a dabchick. Ever afterwards, the inhabitants of Aldbourne were known as 'Aldbourne dabchicks'.

There was great rivalry between Aldbourne and the neighbouring parish of Ramsbury. The traditional Aldbourne Feast, held on or near the feast day of St Mary Magdalen, to whom the parish church is dedicated, generally ended in a free fight between Aldbourne men and intruders from Ramsbury. Ramsbury folk, too, enjoyed playing tricks on the Aldbourne carrier, who served both villages. One of the greatest insults was to tie a dead dabchick to the tail of the carrier's cart and to run behind shouting, 'Yah! Aldbourne dabchick! Yah! Aldbourne dabchick!' Ramsbury villagers, incidentally, would be in a better position than those of Aldbourne to secure a supply of dead dabchicks, for the river Kennet flows nearby.

It sounds odd and trivial, but the association between Aldbourne and the dabchick is evidently old and important. An extraordinary fact is that some of the earliest bells, made in Aldbourne – and Aldbourne was noted for them – bear the engraving of a small, long-necked bird which is undoubtedly supposed to be a dabchick. These bells date from the reign of James I. Aldbourne also possessed a ducking ceremony. Before anyone could call himself an Aldbourne dabchick he had to be ducked in the same tiny pond.

Not many miles away Stratton St Margaret has a story which seems to hint at a similar significance. Someone returning home from the inn raised the alarm because he saw a crocodile climbing out of a ditch. When his neighbours assembled armed with sticks, they found it was only an old scarf. Thereafter Stratton people were known as 'crocodiles'.

5 More Festivals

IN THIS CHAPTER we follow the year through and discover the excuses that Wiltshire villagers in times past used, to take a holiday from work and celebrate.

Shrove Tuesday was in mediaeval times a day of revelry, before the austere weeks of Lent. In that Victorian hotch-potch of antiquities, Chambers' *Book of Days* an account is given of a custom known as 'Lent Crocking', said to be observed in Dorset and Wiltshire.

The boys go round in small parties, headed by a leader, who goes up and knocks at the door, leaving his followers behind him, armed with a good stock of potsherds – the collected relics of the washing-pans, jugs, dishes and plates, that have become the victims of concussion in the hands of unlucky or careless housewives for the past year. When the door is opened, the hero – who is perhaps a farmer's boy, with a pair of black eyes sparkling under the tattered brim on his brown milking-hat – hangs down his head, and, with one corner of his mouth turned up in an irrepressible smile pronounces the following lines:–

> A-shrovin, a-shrovin,
> I be come a-shrovin;
> A piece of bread, a piece of cheese,
> A bit of your fat bacon,
> Or a dish of dough-nuts,
> All of your own makin!
> A-shrovin, a-shrovin,
> I be come a-shrovin,
> Nice meat in a pie,
> My mouth is very dry!
> I wish a wuz zoo well-a-wet
> I'd zing the louder for a nut!
> *Chorus*
> A-shrovin, a-shrovin,
> We be come a-shrovin.

Sometimes he gets a bit of bread and cheese, and at some houses he is told to be gone; in which latter case, he calls up his followers to send their missiles in a rattling broadside against the door. It is rather remarkable that, in Prussia, and perhaps other parts of central Europe, the throwing of broken crockery at doors is a regular practice at marriages.

Edith Olivier records a similar rhyme from Berwick St James:

> Please, ma'am, I've come a-shroving,
> For a piece of pancake,
> Or a little chuckle cheese
> Of your own making.
> Is the piece hot?
> Is the piece cold?
> Is the piece in the pot
> Nine days old?

The last four lines sound like a version of the old nursery rhyme usually rendered:

> Pease pudding hot,
> Pease pudding cold,
> Pease pudding in the pot,
> Nine days old.

The children of Berwick St James used to join hands and go up to the Manor to get a penny each and apples all round. Then they went all round the village.

A dozen or so miles west, south of Warminster, a largely different song was noted down in 1899:

> Dame, is your pan hot?
> Lard and corn is dear;
> I've come a-shroving,
> Tis but once a year.
> So up to the flitch,
> And cut a girt stitch;
> If your hens don't lay,
> I'll steal your cock away
> Before next Shrove Tuesday

A rhyme from Winterbourne Stoke, also collected by Edith Olivier, was rather different:

> Shrove Tuesday, Ash Wednesday, poor Jack* went to
> plough;
> His mother made pancakes – she didn't know how.
> She tossed them, she turned them, she made them so black;
> She put so much pepper, she poisoned poor Jack.

The first four lines of the Shroving Song remembered at Stockton, which is only about four miles from Berwick St James are the same as the Berwick St James version, except that the cheese is a 'truckle' cheese. The second stanza runs:

> Is the knives an forks put?
> Is the bread and cheese cut?
> Is the best barrel tapped?
> For I've come a-shroving.

An identical verse, except that in the third line were the words 'She tipped them, she tossed them', used to be sung at

Trowbridge, and the boys and girls accompanied themselves with it when playing 'Thread the needle'. The same Shrove Tuesday custom was observed at Longbridge Deverill, though the words are not on record. It was the only day in the year when boys and girls played together.

The practical purpose behind Shrovetide customs was to use up foodstuffs which were forbidden by the Church during Lent. There was also a natural desire to have a good feast on this, the last possible opportunity before the Easter season.

Towards the end of the bleak Lenten period, Palm Sunday offered a welcome relief from austerity. It was a popular date for fairs, and Wiltshire had several. We have already described (p.23) one held on Silbury Hill. Another, on the top of Martinsell Hill, was attended by the people of Wootton Rivers and other neighbouring parishes. Men from the neighbouring district used to settle their quarrels by fighting. An unusual pastime followed by the boys was sliding down the hillside, using horses' jawbones like toboggan. Oranges for which the boys scrambled were also thrown down the slope.

Another feature of the Martinsell Fair was the playing of a peculiar form of the game of 'bandy', a kind of hockey recorded mainly in the Midlands and South-West. Boys and young men were stationed, with their hockey sticks, at intervals obliquely up the north slope of the hill, and the ball was hit from one to another to the top. Similar games were played on Roundway Hill, near Devizes, and on Cow Down, Longbridge Deverill. The hill slope at Longbridge Deverill was known as 'Jacob's Ladder', and the game was called 'trap'. One day the players were frightened by a black dog, whom they took to be the Devil, and this put an end to the games. A custom which probably persisted after this was for women and children to go into the fields, 'to tread the wheat'.

Martinsell Fair was discontinued in about 1860, and after that the day was marked by a religious service on the hill.

At about the same time the Palm Sunday gathering on Bidcombe Hill, apparently connected with maintaining the bounds, also lapsed, This was evidently a less spectacular event, though an interesting custom was observed at a depression called The Furmety Hole. Furmety is a kind of wheaten porridge which people used to eat while sitting round the Hole. About twenty miles north-east at Swallowhead Springs, one of the sources of the Kennet, a different culinary custom was observed. As recounted by Long in 1858, sugar was mixed with water from the spring and consumed with cakes and figs. (See also p.23, for a somewhat similar custom on Silbury.)

Another Palm Sunday fair was held on Long Knoll, the big hill near Maiden Bradley. Here again a feature of the celebrations, remembered by villagers in the 1930s, was a ball game always played on the occasion.

Maiden Bradley has memories of several old games, including one with the intriguing name of Bumball Toopey, though this is mentioned in connection with the village pubs rather than as an outdoor sport. Maiden Bradley also had a Village Dance, which was not confined to any particular occasion but was performed at any suitable village event. In my book *A Family and a Village* I give the following account of what took place at Pitton.

Band practices were held in the school. On summer evenings at seven o'clock the Band would line up at the school and then march in procession around the village. They would finish in the meadow opposite the school, where council houses now stand, and play there under the giant elm. They usually had a good audience. Young people would take off their shoes and dance barefoot on the daisies.

I think it likely that the steps of the dance were impromptu. Some village bands, however, knew traditional tunes that had been handed down from previous generations, and in some instances, perhaps at Maiden Bradley, traditional dances may have been attached to them.

Another spring-time festival, this one centring on the church, was known as 'clipping the church'. Parishioners assembled in the churchyard and, holding hands, formed a ring around the church, which was thus entirely enclosed. A short dance was then performed. Most churches would need a larger congregation than they normally get nowadays to engage in this ceremony. In some instances, however, it was performed by schoolchildren. That was so at Bradford-on-Avon, where until about the middle of the nineteenth century it was kept up on Shrove Tuesday. Other

Wiltshire places with which it was associated are Warminster and Trowbridge.

It is recorded that the village of Tilshead once possessed parish officials known as 'tutti-men'. No details survive of their function, which must, however, have been similar to that of the 'tutti-men' of Hungerford, in Berkshire, who attend the Town Constable for traditional festivities at Hock-tide. In passing, it is interesting to note that Tilshead is recorded in the Domesday Book (1086) as having sixty-six burgesses, which would make it one of the largest boroughs in the county. It must have been the centre of an enormous sheep trade.

Hock-tide and tutti-men are associated with the administration of common rights, a matter which must at one time have been of importance to every Wiltshire parish. At present about fifty surviving commons are listed for the county, though the name 'Common' survives also in connection with many lands now enclosed. Some of these commons are nowadays controlled by parish councils or parish meetings, some by the lords of local manors, some by trustees, and some by committees of the commoners. Cricklade, which still possesses a small common, had from ancient times a Court Leet, consisting of a jury of twelve commoners who met once a year to administer the parish common lands. Presumably these were then much more extensive than they are now, for every householder once had the right to turn nine head of cattle to graze the common lands from August to February and thirty sheep from September to February. That arrangement left the summer free, and one of the chief duties of the Court Leet was to let out the commons for summer grazing and haymaking.

The custom of letting out grassland for summer use only is still common in Somerset and certain other western counties but survives in only a few places in Wiltshire. Wishford, for one, keeps up an ancient custom whereby the grazing and haying rights on two water-meadows are sold by auction annually. The sale takes place in the church porch, just before sunset on Rogation Monday. Buyers are summoned by the ringing of the church bell a quarter of an hour before sunset. They arrive to find the parish clerk marching up and down the church path, carrying the key of the church. The auction, conducted by the clerk, begins at five minutes to sunset.

Precisely at sunset the grass is sold to the last bidder, the auctioneer concluding the deal by striking a stone of the church gatepost with his key. The name attached to this sale is 'Midsummer Tithes', although the sale takes place at Rogationtide, which is in May.

Rogationtide services in rural parishes are a custom which lapsed for a time and were revived after the second world war in many Wiltshire villages. The usual procedure is for Church of England and Nonconformist congregations to unite for an evening service which begins at one place of worship and ends at another. In between the congregation in procession visits selected stations, such as the village green, a farmyard, the school, the village hall, a garden and the churchyard. Prayers are said, a lesson read and hyms sung at each station.

This comes somewhere near the original purpose of Rogationtide, which was 'a perambulation or beating of the parish bounds'. It was a means of teaching the people the parish boundaries before the days of Ordnance Survey. A record of 1669 describes the beating of the bounds of the parish of Everley. I know of no Gospel Oaks in the county – a name given to trees which served as landmarks and at which the lessons were read on the Rogationtide perambulations.

Miss Olivier records some amusing details of the ceremony of beating the bounds as practised at Maiden Bradley 'during the last quarter of a century', which would be since 1900.

A trap, laden with drinks and eatables, was driven along the boundary line. If a stranger were seen coming along the road a halt was made, a cross 'hooked out' with a spud on the wayside waste, and the stranger was invited to have a drink and a feed. If he innocently partook of the repast he had to face the penalty of being stood upon his head and well beaten with the shovel. Once silk-workers going from the Deverills to the silk-works at Mere were molested in this manner in such a rough and unbecoming way that trouble resulted, which terminated only by profuse apologies from the Estate agent.

Most midsummer activities died out long ago, but John Powell recorded in 1894 how Hill Deverill parishioners used to go to the churchyard on 'Midsummer Night' looking for ghosts. Men without heads had been seen, as well as a little child and 'a turr'ble sight o' galleysome (fearsome) things'. The parish was very isolated and became accessible by road only in 1854. His informant remembered going as a boy, in about 1833, 'to see them come out and in', and in particular to look for the ghost of his 'butty'.

The word 'butty' is interesting, and in this case meant his former companion in fieldwork. In the last century it was in wide usage for 'work-mate' or 'friend', though it has now, where it persists, given way to the American 'buddy' This is supposed to derive from 'brother', as it used to be pronounced in transatlantic English, but an origin in 18th or 19th century colloquial English is just as likely. In this country, 'butty' is believed to come from the Romany *booty-pal,* a fellow workman.

The Cricklade Bark Harvest Festival was an anomalous celebration which seems to have been an end-of-season feast, much like a Harvest Home, given by the local tanneries to mark the end of the bark harvest. It was marked by plenty of good food and ale and conviviality.

Miss Edith Olivier, noted down at least a part of a play performed at the Cricklade Bark Harvest Festival. Apparently it was also performed as a Mumming Play at Christmas. It was called *The Shepherd and the Maiden,* and here is the text:

SHEPHERD: Once I was made a shepherd on the plains,
Courting my shepherdess among the swains;
But now a courting life I'll bid adieu,
And a more melancholy way pursue.
The shade my coverlet, the bank my bed,
Where on the flowery pillows I lay my head;
My mates the fruits that grow about the field,
My drink the tears my eyes in sorrow yield.
But, ah! who comes? What shining beauty's this?
Disturbs my solitude and shady bliss?

MAIDEN: I am one that is lost in a wilderness of care,
Where I find nothing to prevent despair;
I am a harmless damsel wandering on the plain;
I'm lost and fear I never shall be found again.
Look here, look there; there's nothing to be seen
But woods, and groves, and meadows all in green;
I am so thirsty that I scarce can speak.

SHEPHERD: Must she grieve thus and not my heart-strings
break?
She sees me not; then I'll accost her first.
Pray, take this bottle and so quench your thirst.

MAIDEN: It's good, indeed; but you much better be,
For being so courteous as to give it me.

SHEPHERD: Had I a more worthy gift, to call it mine,
Proud would I be, dear maid, to name it thine.

MAIDEN: Thou art more worthy than all gifts beside.
Ask what thou wilt, it shall not be denied.

SHEPHERD: Then speak I will, by such fair promise led.
What I shall ask is for thyself to wed.

MAIDEN: Since lost I was about this woody ground,
Receive me here, and keep what thou hast found;
Come, lead me forward to my father's court,
And we'll grace our nuptials with some friendly
sport.

The play compares unfavourably with the Mumming Play
on pages 68-73. The Mumming Play, with lines that do not
scan, unintelligible words, gaps in the flow of ideas, and
indications of patching and additions at various times seems
genuinely old. By contrast, the Bark Festival Play text was
obviously written by a person of some education and with
pretensions to being a poet.

The Tanbark Festival, to give it yet another of its names,
superficially resembles the Tan Hill Fair, named after the hill
on which it is held. In fact, there is no real connection, any
more than there is between Tan Hill and the Celtic
mythological figure, Tana. Popular belief, presumably
deriving from the speculation of antiquarians, imagines the
hill as named after a Celtic fire-god, an argument evidently
stemming from *tan*, the word for fire in Old Welsh. But the
alternative name, apparently in earlier usage, is St Anne's
Hill, still the formal name of the site, and the date of the fair, 6
August, seems to link it with St Anne's Day (old style). The
church at All Cannings, nearby, is dedicated to the same
saint.

I have references to three other summer feasts in Wiltshire
villages. One was at East Harnham, at an unspecified date in
July. There were music and dancing, and the dinner was

evidently attended by many of the most important tradesmen of Salisbury. The festival was continued until about the middle of the nineteenth century, but its purpose and history are unrecorded.

Stockton feast began on the first Sunday after 6 July and continued for a whole week. Many of the villagers apparently used the occasion to sell 'sweets, cakes, ginger beer and other fairings' from roadside stalls, while 'five or six of the villagers got temporary licences for the week and sold beer from their own houses'. It seems to have been a very gay occasion, but again its purpose and history are not known.

Crockerton Revel is better documented and took place on the Sunday following 7 July – the date commemorating the Translation of Thomas à Becket. St Becket's Day festivals, as once they were called, were forbidden in 1538, but a few survived. Records of Crockerton Revel, dating from the 1890s, imply that it was still current, accompanied by an attractive local legend. Thomas à Becket 'used to come to Crockerton Revel dressed like a gentleman, and he would depart through the wood dressed like a beggar, in rags, having spent all his money at the Revel'. Longbridge Deverill church, nearby, was supposed to have been consecrated by him.

Tan Hill Fair brings us to Lammas-tide, around 1 August. Lammas is a corruption of 'Loaf-Mass', according to most authorities, though some prefer to derive the name from the Celtic festival Lugnasad, which was doubtless the origin of many of the customs. Lammas Fairs, particularly for the dispersal of sheep, were held in many parts of the country, though Wiltshire apparently had few. One at Cricklade was held on the first Sunday after 12 August. Among the old sports engaged in on that occasion were bull-baiting, boxing, 'wrestling matches', hack-swording, kick-shins – which means exactly what it says!, 'break heads' – played with hefty cudgels – and cock-fighting. The date was also the occasion when the commoners were allowed their cattle out for free grazing.

Britford Fair, also on 12 August, was within my own time one of the biggest fairs in the south of England. It was devoted almost entirely to sheep. Here is a personal reminiscence of the Fair, taken from an old book of mine, *Peasant's Heritage* (written in the 1930s).

When we emerged into the wide highway of Exeter Street (Salisbury) a curious and somewhat uncanny sight met our eyes. Before and behind us, as far as the eye could penetrate through the faintly-lit gloom (for this was about three o'clock in the morning), were sheep. Hundreds of thousands of them in a bobbing, jostling, steaming multitude, they trotted steadily through the silent city with only the glimmer of a street lamp here and there to light their way, while the vague, column spire of the cathedral loomed overhead, just perceptible against the dusky sky.

We were more than an hour and a half traversing the mile or so between Salisbury and Britford. The entire length of the road was packed with sheep, there being only about ten yards interval between each flood.

Warminster had a sheep fair on 11 August; Highworth Fair was on 13 August; and Trowbridge used to have a three-day fair from 5 August.

Customs concerning harvest are dealt with in a later chapter. On the arable farms of Wiltshire harvest was the great divide of the year. Brought up on such a farm, I remember that up to about the end of July the farm routine proceeded, undisturbed. The few cows were milked at the appointed times and taken to and from their pastures; the shepherd idled away his time, watching the sheep on the downs; the last acres of hoeing were dealt with; women and old men pottered around the fields with thistle-paddles, removing thistles and docks. On Saturday afternoons I played cricket with the village team.

Then harvest started, and I saw no more cows or sheep. The root fields had to take their chance with weeds. No knowledgeable cricket club secretary would arrange any fixtures for August or early September, knowing only too well the impossibility of getting together a team.

From breakfast-time till after dark our life was bounded by the hedges of the harvest field in which we were working. We cut the corn with a binder; we stooked the sheaves; we turned them, unless we were unusually lucky with the weather, half-a-dozen times, to dry out; eventually we carted them and built them into ricks. One rick after another, until twenty or thirty were standing in the rick-yards. We heard no radio, saw no papers, were unaware of any national or international

news. Our only link even with the little world of the village
was the daily arrival of the women at tea-time, with drinks
and eatables loaded on push-chairs and prams. It was a hard
but in a way idyllic life. We were entirely immersed, without
distraction, in the job on hand.

And when it was all over, the summer had slipped away and
we were in the middle of autumn. Pearly mists shrouded the
countryside in the morning. The blackberries and apples were
ripe. Mushrooms could be gathered in the meadows. And the
cricket season had given way to football.

The successful conclusion of harvest, that testing marathon
completed against the strenuous opposition of the English
weather, was naturally an occasion for great rejoicing. The
last sheaf was hoisted triumphantly on a prong and carried
back to the rick. My father could remember the old Harvest
Shout, though it was not used in my time:

> Well ploughed!
> Well sowed!
> Well harrowed!
> Well mowed!
> And all safely carted to the barn wi' nary a load throwed!
> Hip-hip-hip-hooray!

This spontaneous exuberance led naturally to the Harvest
Home Supper. During and just after the war Harvest Homes
of a sort became quite popular, but these were revivals. In
compiling their village Scrap Book the Alderbury Women's
Institute were able only to say that an old man who died
before the 1939-45 war, aged ninety, could remember when
Harvest Homes were celebrated. My father used to tell me
tales of Harvest Homes, though whether they were his
personal memories or retailed second-hand I am not sure.
Anyway, they would belong to the second half of the
nineteenth century.

There was the tale of the farmer who made the finest and
most highly applauded Harvest Home speech ever recorded.
He climbed to his feet, banged the table for silence, cleared his
throat and spoke. 'Knock the bung in thik other cider barrel',
he said. Then he sat down, amid rapturous applause.

I heard too of the cornet player who, when the village band
played at Harvest Homes, used to request, 'Thee prop I up

somewhere so's I can't vall over, and I'll keep playing for ee.'
One evening he was wedged between sacks against the big
barn doors when someone took the peg out behind him and he
disappeared, with a final discordant flourish, into the night.

And there was the teetotal farmer whose Harvest Home was
remembered in verse by the village poet, who wrote a song
with the refrain:

> And there stood our glasses with water so clear,
> But all the cry was, We wanted some beer!

Harvest Homes were clearly convivial affairs.

So highly was the sheep, 'The Golden Hoof', regarded on
the arable farms that it was said that the farms were run for
the sheep's benefit. The shepherd was the aristocrat of farm
workers. His colleagues noted with envy and some resentment
the easy life he had, following his flock on the downs, while
they were sweating away, harvesting. Harvest meant little in
the shepherd's calendar, and so sheep fairs continued to be
held, as need arose, thoughout August and September.

One of Marlborough's great sheep fairs was held on 22
August. Bradford-on-Avon had a fair on 24 August; Swindon
on 11 September; and Wilton's great autumn fair, one of the
largest in the West of England, on 12 September. In the 1860s
90,000 to 100,000 sheep were sold annually at Wilton's
September Fair.

Wilton Fair used to be the scene of a contest to determine
who would bear the title of 'King of the Shepherds' for the
coming year. It was held at the Wheatsheaf Inn, Wilton,
where the shepherds put up for the night, and took the form of
a 'great fight', but with what weapons is not recorded. 'That
night the shepherds slept on the floor of the Inn in a rough
circle, each with his head on his dog for a pillow. Thus the
shepherd guarded his dog, which was his most valuable
property, and the dog guarded his master's small belongings.'
A great-uncle of mine, however, who was a shepherd, had a
dog which he sold regularly at Wilton Fair. He knew it would
find its way home again within a few weeks!

So the year moved on to Michaelmas, with its fairs and the
changing of farm tenancies. At least, that has been the
significance of Michaelmas all my lifetime, but apparently it
was not always so. Thomas Davis, of Longleat, who in 1794

prepared one of the earliest of all surveys of Wiltshire agriculture for the newly-formed Board of Agriculture, wrote:

> The old custom of South Wilts was almost invariabley a Lady-day's entry [to a farm tenancy]. Indeed a Michaelmas one was not at all adapted to the customs of feeding the commonable lands of the district . . . The reason appears to be this; the basis of all agreements for renting land is, that every renter shall have a complete year's produce for a year's rent . . . The year's commonage was only complete when there was nothing left on the land for the cattle to eat; and (on that account, perhaps,) our forefathers fixed on Lady-day for the commencement of their year, not only in their agricultural but also in their civil establishment . . . South Wiltshire, as one of the last districts to retain its common rights, observes the custom of a Lady-day entry wherever those rights exist . . .

He goes on to explain that under this system the retiring tenant still harvests all corn sown before Lady-day, whether in the spring or in the previous autumn. On the other hand, the new tenant takes possession of the water-meadows, which have to be irrigated to produce early spring grass, at the previous Christmas. The new tenant is also allowed the outgoing tenant's last spring crop with grass, if he so wishes. The old tenant keeps part of the house and stables, while the new tenant has the other part.

'The old tenant', says Davis, 'likewise keeps the barns till that time, to thrash out his corn, the new tenant not wanting them till the ensuing harvest, except at sheep-shearing, when they are open to him. In this intermixed state, the two families live for upwards of a year.'

It is to be hoped that they remained good friends. One sees ample scope for dispute and friction. Here again we notice that the sheep and their needs are dominant. Grazing takes priority over crop-growing. When the pendulum moved in favour of arable farming, a Michaelmas tenancy became more convenient.

Michaelmas in the old days was therefore not so much the occasion for farm sales as for the continuing series of fairs for the dispersal of livestock and for the exchange of farm labourers. Michaelmas was the recognised season for changing jobs. Contracts were struck between employer and man, normally for a year; these were usually made at fairs around Michaelmas, which therefore became known as Hiring Fairs. Another name for them is Mop Fairs. Christina Hole, in *English Custom and Usage,* notes that servants looking for posts 'stood in a row wearing the signs of their trade, a crook or tuft of wool for a shepherd, a whip for a carter, straw for a cowman, and so on. On being engaged, they were given a 'fastenpenny' or earnest-money, and the rest of the day was spent in enjoying themselves at the fair.' Domestic servants paraded holding a mop, hence the name.

Today it sounds like a harmless and desirable break in the monotony and grind of the year's labours, but it did not appear that way to all of our forefathers. Francis Heath, in a book written in 1883 entitled *Peasant Life in the West of England,* looking back over the changes of the previous decades, declared:

> The 'mop', 'hiring' or 'statute' fair, to which no reference has yet been made, had not ceased to disgrace some of the smaller towns of the western districts. These fairs, annually held to enable servants of both sexes to be hired, were, oftentimes, the occasion of the greatest drunkenness and profligacy. Young girls dressed in their finest clothes were exhibited like cattle to be hired by the would-be employers, who came to the fair to seek their services; and the scenes which frequently took place at the close of the day were too disgraceful for description. But, though the 'mop' fair had not then, as it has not yet, become an institution of the past, there were happily signs that its decline had commenced.'

Wootton Bassett Fair, on the first Tuesday of October, was associated with a very ancient ceremony known as the 'Word Ale'. The participants were tenants of the Lord of the Manor of Wootton Bassett, each tenant taking it in turn to act as host. The ostensible purpose of the celebration. which was held in secret, was to secure exemption from the payment of tithes. Prayers were said for the Cistercian monks who, back in the twelfth century, had granted such exemption to any tenants observing the custom. Hymns were also sung and large quantities of ale consumed. The event was recorded by cutting a notch in a yard-long hazel wand, which was then handed to the tenant who had to act as host for next year. The custom was kept up till towards the end of the nineteenth century.

The Michaelmas fairs of late September and early October lead on to the late October fairs, which more or less coincide with Hallowe'en, All Saints' Day and the Celtic feast of Samhain. Wiltshire fairs of that period included Salisbury on 22 October (this is now primarily a pleasure fair, perpetuated by travelling showmen); Hindon on 29 October; Warminster on the 26th; Devizes on the 20th; and Chippenham on the 29th. Marlborough had a fair on 23 November, which is perhaps a bit late to have any connection with Samhain, though if we remember to deduct eleven days for the change in the calendar it is close. The dates of these events, however, seem to be their only possible connection with the ancient Samhain or Hallowe'en celebrations. The fairs themselves followed a conventional pattern.

The bonfires which were traditionally associated with the festival have been transferred to 5 November. Bonfire Night parties are still held in most Wiltshire towns and villages. In my native village of Pitton we had a traditional hill-top site for the village bonfire. There was a general belief, entirely unfounded, among young people in the 1920s and 1930s that we were free to do whatever we liked on that night, regardless of the policeman; hence, stealing besoms to use as torches, building faggot barriers across roads and starting additional bonfires in unauthorised places were a usual feature of Guy Fawkes' Night.

Samhain was also the traditional period for the slaughter of animals, a seasonal event which was paralleled until recent years in the killing of the cottage or farmhouse pig. Until the 1930s most Wiltshire villages had an official pig-killer, who was extremely busy at this season, most cottagers keeping a pig in a garden sty.

Late autumn was, of course, the natural season for killing pigs. Not only did they represent a store of meat for the winter but also food to feed them was growing scarce by November. During the summer, when they were growing fast, the refuse from the cottage garden provided much of their diet; and after harvest barley meal, ground from the gleanings of the harvest-field, served to fatten them. In November they were at their best.

I often served as assistant (unpaid) to my father when he was the village pig-killer. Although he held that post chiefly because no-one else was willing to take on the job, his position was, to a certain extent, official, in that his appointment was duly recorded in the minutes of the village Pig Club. Virtually all cottagers belonged to the Club, which was an insurance society. Each member paid, if I remember rightly, sixpence per pig and was entitled to full value of any pig that died (provided there was enough money in the funds at the time!). My father's fee for killing a pig was, I believe, half-a-crown, plus the offal. If the owner kept the offal for his own use, he paid extra for the killing.

In my time the pig was killed by humane-killer, but not much earlier it had its throat cut, while strong men held it down. An elderly lady, Lizzie Collins, who was expert at making black puddings, came and caught the blood, which was generally recognised as her perquisite, though goodness knows why. Perhaps it was because she used to help my mother with the subsequent processing of the offal.

After death, the pig was singed over a straw fire; then, while the skin was still hot, the toughest bristles were scraped off with a pewter candlestick. Later we used kitchen knives, but a pewter candlestick was the traditional tool. Overnight it was hung from a beam in a barn, by means of a gamril inserted under the sinews of its hind legs. Before it was left for the night, with a sack tied around its snout to protect it from cats, it was disembowelled. The offal was carried home to the waiting women, who had before them a busy evening, cleaning chitterlings, allocating the choice portions of liver, tongue, heart, melt and so on to sundry relations and friends, stripping off fat for lard, and making faggots.

Later, after a few joints had been set aside for fresh meat, the greater part of the carcase was salted down, either as ham or bacon. Many cottagers possessed silts, often of wood but quite frequently lined with lead, in which the bacon was set to mature in a bed of salt. I think most of the lead silts must must have been surrendered for scrap metal during the second world war. When the bacon was thoroughly cured it was placed on a bacon rack of wood, which was tacked to the great beam in the kitchen. Our bacon rack was always well stocked with sides of bacon all through the winter when I was a boy. The hams were hung in the open chimney, where they got well smoked. Towards the end of the winter a layer of rancid fat which covered the bacon had to be cut away before the meat was used, but under that the bacon was always wholesome. Some of the pigs were huge, and usually they were much fatter than we like them nowadays, but villagers of previous generations tended to be starved of fat and could not get too much of it.

Pig-killing time was a busy period for my father, who sometimes had to kill five or six a week. It was made more hectic by the convention that a pig must be killed when the moon was waxing, otherwise the meat would go bad. My father himself did not subscribe to this belief, regarding it as mere superstition, but he had to accept the fact that many of his clients did.

Between the wars an attempt was made to establish a second bonfire night on 11 November, to mark the armistice which ended the 1914-18 war. The date coincided approximately with Martinmas, which, like Hallowe'en, was anciently associated with the slaughter of livestock for winter provisions. The idea did not, however, catch on.

We are now getting near to the season of Christmas. Although Santa Claus is now synonymous with Father Christmas, the original St Nicholas had his feast day on 6 December. To that day belongs the curious ceremony of electing a boy bishop, a custom once widespread throughout England. At Salisbury it can be traced back to 1319. The boy bishop was elected from among their number by the Cathedral choristers and held office from St Nicholas' Day to 28 December, the Feast of the Holy Innocents.

> He was duly invested in all the proper vestments of a bishop, while a number of his companions were suitably robed to attend him as priests and deacons . . . During the tenure of the office the boy bishop performed all the functions of the actual dignitary, holding a visitation, singing vespers and other offices, appointing to any prebend that fell vacant, and even singing some imitation of the mass.

Should the boy die during his term of office he was buried with all the honours due to a bishop, and a tomb with a miniature effigy of a bishop in Salisbury Cathedral is said to be that of a boy, though without, it seems, much justification. The practice was frowned upon by ecclesiastical authorities during the Middle Ages, and several church councils passed laws against it. In England it survived until suppressed by law by Henry VIII, but Henry's daughter, Mary, revived the custom. We are told that in 1555 'the child bishop of Paules Church, with his company, were admitted into the queen's privy chamber, where he sang before her on Saint Nicholas' Day and upon Holy Innocents' Day' (Joseph Strutt, *Sports and Pastimes of the People of England*). He added: 'After the death of Mary this silly mummery was totally discontinued.'

Although Christmas mumming plays have apparently died out in Wiltshire, and there is always the chance that some may be resurrected, many villages have recollections of them. Edith Olivier in the 1930s found traces in Amesbury, Maiden Bradley, Horningsham, Cricklade, Wootton Rivers, Woodford and Quidhampton. I also heard references at Stockton and Winterslow; and Canute, Helon, Peacock, *English Ritual Drama* note that Mumming plays were extant, at the dates given, at the following places: All Cannings (1868), Avebury (1852), Baydon, Buttermere (c.1880), Chilton Foliat (1901), Highworth, Hilmarton, Inglesham (c.1840), Lydiard Millicent, Marlborough, Minety (1876), Netheravon (c.1901), Potterne (1890), Rushall (c.1890), Salisbury (before 1875), Shrewton (1936), South Marston, Stourton, Stratton St Margaret (before 1912), Swindon (c.1835), Wootton Bassett (c.1860). In 1930 it was reported that the Alton Barnes Christmas mumming play was performed annually, and the Shrewton Christmas mumming play was reported extant in 1936.

Many of these places now preserve few details of their mumming plays. Winterslow has recorded the recollection that mummers from the village used to visit Old Lodge Farm, several miles away on the downs towards Idmiston, at Christmastime. The last of the Winterslow mummers, Ernest Judd, died only a few years ago at the age of 99. Wootton Rivers preserves the words of one of the mummers' songs. In Cricklade and Woodford little remains except the memory that those places once had mummers.

About some of the others, however, more information is available, and Edith Olivier has preserved for us the complete dialogue of the Quidhampton Mummers' Play, which I here give. She commented that:

This version of the Mumming Play was passed down verbally through generations of Quidhampton Mummers and was last performed in 1913. It is now written down for the first time, at the actual dictation of some of the last of the Mummers. Each man had only learnt his own part, and none of them had even a scrap of paper with which to refresh his memory after all these years. The Mummers were most careful to recite the words *as they had heard them,* without any attempt to alter them if they were incomprehensible. Mr Cousins (who as a boy used to go about with the Mummers, helping to carry their properties) was able in most cases to piece the parts together, and so to recall the shape of this very ancient play.

The Quidhampton Mummers' Play

Characters

BOLD SOLDIER *(wears an old military tunic)*
FATHER CHRISTMAS *(Traditional dress. Carries a broomstick with a bunch of holly and mistletoe on it)*
KING GEORGE *(Domed hat)*
TURKISH KNIGHT *(A little smoking cap with tassel)*
CUT-THE-DASH *(A sash worn across his chest)*
THE DOCTOR *(Black clothes; dress coat; cocked hat with feathers)*
LITTLE JOHNNY JACK *(Seven dolls hung across his back). All the characters have their clothes sewn all over with different coloured cambric, slashed into ribands*

Enter BOLD SOLDIER

BOLD SOLDIER: Ah ha! The doors are open and we're now in.
We beg your favour for to win.
For whether we rise or whether we fall,
We'll do our best endeavour to please you all.
We're none of the ragged tribe, ladies and gentlemen.
We're come here to show you a little fight and pastime.
And if you don't believe the words I say,
Walk in, Father Christmas, and clear the way.
Retires. Enter FATHER CHRISTMAS

FATHER CHRISTMAS: In comes I, Father Christmas.
Christmas or Christmas not.
I hope old Father Christmas will never be forgot.
And now I pray you, Ladies and Gentlemen,
To give us room to render.
For we're come here to show you fight,
To pass away the winter.
A fight you've never seen before.
I'm the man that leads King George in the door.
Walk in, King George, act thy way, and show thy part,
And show the beloved company of thy wondrous art.

KING GEORGE enters

KING GEORGE: In comes I, King George, lately come from town to town,
To show the greatness of my strength,
To show the feat of valour.
Dun cow and dun,
Likewise of men's chastity.
To see two dragons fight.
And to kill an ugly creature
Is all my delight.
Ask for Bold Soldier. Oft of him I've been told.
I wish his ugly face I could now behold.'

FATHER CHRISTMAS: Walk in, Bold Soldier, cut thy way and act thy part,
And show the beloved company of thy wondrous art.

Enter BOLD SOLDIER

BOLD SOLDIER: In comes I, Bold Soldier, Bold Slasher is my name.
Tis I that fought the fiery dragon
And brought him to his slaughter,
And by that means I won the King of Egypt's daughter.
My head is bound with iron, and my body bound with steel,
And with my arms up to my knuckle bones
I'll fight King George to win his throne.
Pull out thy purse and pay;
Pull out thy sword and slay.

Satisfaction will I have of thee before I go away.

KING GEORGE: No purse will I pull out,
No money will I pay.
Neither shall thee give me satisfaction
Before thee'st go away.

They fight. Bold Soldier drops wounded

FATHER CHRISTMAS: O King, O King, what hast thou done?
See, one of my soldiers lies bleeding on the ground.

KING GEORGE: You gave me the first offer, Daddy, how could I refuse it?
Have you got another of your soldiers for me to conquer or kill?

FATHER CHRISTMAS: Yes, I've another of my soldiers for thee to conquer or kill.
Walk in, the Turkish Knight,
Go thy way and act thy part,
And show the beloved company of thy wondrous art.

Enter the TURKISH KNIGHT

TURKISH KNIGHT: In comes I, the Turkish Knight,
Come from a foreign land to fight,
I'll fight this English champion bold,
If his blood runs hot, I'll quickly draw it cold.

KING GEORGE: O Turk, O Turk! thou talkest bold.
Thou talkest as other Turks, as I've been told.
Pull out thy purse and pay,
Pull out thy sword and slay.
Satisfaction will I have of thee before thee'st go away.

TURKISH KNIGHT: No purse will I pull out,
No money will I pay.
Neither shall I give thee satisfaction
Before I go away.

They fight. Turkish Knight drops wounded

FATHER CHRISTMAS: O King, O King, what hast thou done?
See, one of my soldiers lies bleeding on the ground.

KING GEORGE: You gave me the first offer, Daddy, how could I refuse it?
Have you got another of your soldiers for me to conquer or to kill?

FATHER CHRISTMAS: Yes, I've got another of my soldiers for
thee to conquer or to kill.
Walk in, Cut-the-Dash.
Go thy way and act thy part,
And show the beloved company of thy wondrous
art.

Enter CUT-THE-DASH

CUT-THE-DASH: In comes I, Cut-the-Dash,
With my broadsword and my fine sash.
Although my king is not here to take his part,
I'll take it with all my heart.
Now I've almost end my ditty,
I hope on me you'll all have pity.
Now I've almost end my story,
I hope the battle will end in glory.

They fight. He goes on his knees, not altogether beaten

CUT-THE-DASH: I'll have no more of thy high words, nor none
of thy diddly dumps.
For now that thee'st cut my legs off, I'll fight thee
on my stumps!

*They fight again. King George wins. The three lie on the floor. King
George walks round them*

KING GEORGE: Behold and see the wonders I have done!
I've cut down my enemies like the evening sun.
(to FATHER CHRISTMAS): Call for a doctor as quick as you
please!
Perhaps one of his pills may give a little ease.

FATHER CHRISTMAS: Is there a doctor to be found
To cure my three sons which lie bleeding on the
ground?

Enter DOCTOR

DOCTOR: Yes, there is a doctor to be found
To cure thy three sons which lie bleeding on the
ground.

FATHER CHRISTMAS: Are you he?

DOCTOR: I am that.

FATHER CHRISTMAS: What's thy fee, doctor?

DOCTOR: Ten pound is my fee.
But full fifty will I have of thee,
Before I set thy three sons free.

FATHER CHRISTMAS: Tut, tut, Doctor; none of thee foreign
off talk.

DOCTOR: Yes, Father Christmas, I am a foreign off man.
I've travelled India, South India and Bendigo,
And now I've returned to England again.
FATHER CHRISTMAS: Well, give us a sample of thee work.
DOCTOR: I carry a little bottle by my side
Which is called the Opliss Popliss Drops,
Which I touch one to the heart and one to the
head.

(He does so)

I heal thee of thy wounds once more,
So please get up, I pray.

*They all get up and mingle together, fighting again, their swords
mingled in a bunch. Father Christmas, with his holly bough, forces
himself in among them*

FATHER CHRISTMAS: I'll have no more of that fighting here.

(Enter JOHNNY JACK)

JOHNNY JACK: Here comes I, little Johnny Jack,
With my wife and family on my back.
Out of eleven I have but seven,
And three of them are gone to heaven.
One to the Workhouse he is gone,
And the rest will go when I get home.
Although I am but short and small,
I think I am the best man among you all.
What say you, Daddy?
FATHER CHRISTMAS: Yes, yes, my son.
JOHNNY JACK: Christmas comes but once a year,
And when it comes it brings good cheer,
Roast beef, plum pudding and mince pie.
Who likes that better than Father Christmas and
I?
Each one of them is a very good thing,
And a pot of your Christmas ale will make our
voices ring.
Right wheel! Quick march!

They march in a circle, with tambourine and concertina

ALL SING: Christmas is the time for merriment,
time for merriment,
time for merriment,
Christmas is the time for merriment,
Christmas is the time!

They stand in a circle and sing

Britannia long expected news from the fleet,
Commanded by Nelson the French to defeat.
But when the news came over, to England it was
layed,
The French were defeated, but Lord Nelson he was
slayed.

They sing other songs, ending with 'God save the King'

Such is the only complete version of the Mumming Play I know of in Wiltshire. The others of which only parts are extant, however, seem to have followed very much the same lines, with slight variations in some of the characters.

In the Horningsham version 'Johnny Jack' is 'Little Man Jack', and his introductory verse runs:

In comes I, Little Man Jack,
A wife and family at my back.
Out of eight I got but five,
And I'm afraid they'll all be starved alive.
Some to the Workhouse they are gone.
The rest will go when I get home.
Although my body is but small,
I'm the biggest rogue among you all.

The plays have clearly been built up and adapted in the course of centuries. The final chorus of the Quidhampton Play obviously belongs to the Napoleonic wars, but one of Cut-the-Dash's speeches is reminiscent of the song about Admiral Benbow, who died in 1702.

Brave Benbow lost his legs,
And all on his stumps he begs,
'Fight on, my English lads;
'Tis our lot.'

The character of the Turkish Knight would seem to date from the Crusades. In some versions two Turkish Knights appear, and it is not clear whether they or St. George are the hero.

Little Johnny Jack, who appears in almost every version of the play, is indeed an important character, for he accounts for the Play's survival. He is unashamedly a beggar, of the type who still in some countries displays his mutilations and starving children and asks for alms. In his concluding speech he directly invites the audience to contribute 'roast beef, plum pudding, mince pie and a pot of your Christmas ale'. He is assisted by Father Christmas who, as Master of Ceremonies, is always conscious of the 'beloved company' for whom they are performing.

Here we have the clue to the successful perpetuation of the Mumming Plays. They gave the hungry poor, in times of austerity and deprivation, as during the Napoleonic Wars, a legitimate opportunity for seeking charity from the rich. They survived not because of an innate interest in folklore or old customs but simply because they were useful. Indeed, the comparative absence of references to mumming plays in the literature of the cultured and fashionable of the eighteenth and early nineteenth centuries suggests that the upper classes regarded these naive efforts of the poor with a benevolent indifference. The poor, however, had a vested interest in keeping them alive. All reminiscences about them speak of the Mummers doing their rounds of the big houses in the neighbourhood.

One interesting incidental piece of information is preserved about the Amesbury Mumming Play. It is remembered that the players had their faces blackened. In surviving versions in some other counties the players wore masks. This seems to relate to an ancient belief that the characters should be entirely absorbed in their parts and consequently unrecognisable.

Teffont Women's Institute records that local people used to go carol-singing around the village, pushing a harmonium on a barrel, but this may or may not be a survival of an old custom. We used to do much the same at Pitton in the 1930s and late 1940s, but simply because we thought it was a good idea for raising money for charity. Carol-singing to the accompaniment of a harmonium or organ carried on a tractor trailer is still practised at Winterslow and probably other villages.

A belief that oxen kneel on the night of the Nativity was once widespread, and Thomas Hardy wrote a poem around it in 1915. Seventeen years earlier John Powell recorded the same opinion in south-west Wiltshire, though he added that it was not then commonly held. His informant, when a boy, had been keen to put it to the test, and stories are told of farm workers who have done so and have been disappointed. Sometimes this has been rationalised by suggesting that cattle still observe the old-style calendar, and a dialect poem from the Gloucestershire side of the county boundary less than a century ago adds firmly that 'the old time is the right'. The original idea comes, according to some, from Jacopo Sannazzaro, a Neapolitan poet whose work was popular in the reigns of Henry VII and Henry VIII.

Another notion, which the faint-hearted surely avoided trying out, was that by standing in the church porch on New Year's Eve you could see the wraiths of those doomed to die in the coming year. If you saw yourself, you would be among them.

In the late 1930s a company of sword dancers, organised by the late Rolf Gardiner at Fontmell Magna, in Dorset, visited a number of Wiltshire towns and villages in an attempt to revive the old Plough Monday festival, but the outbreak of war put an end to the scheme before it could get established.

Many of the feasts we have noted during this survey of the year were known by the alternative name of 'Ales', usually preceded by a description of the relevant season at which they were held, as in 'Whitsun Ales', they were named for beneficiary, as in 'Church Ales'. The derivation of Wootton Bassett's 'Word Ales' is uncertain. 'Church Ales' were normally feasts or festivals organised for the benefit of the church or something connected with it; as, for instance, a regular 'Ale' might be held for the upkeep of a chapel.

A Wiltshire parish which once held Christmas Ales is Everley. In 1610 its Rector wrote:

When I first came to this parish, beinge now about eleven or twelve years past, it was said there had been a custome longe before, of making the neighbourhood eat bread and cheese and drink beer at the parsonage house on Christmas Day after eveninge praier, which custome out of neighbourlie kindnesse, or out of weaknesses (for I misliked it) I continued accordinglie till the Gunpowder Plot 1605. After whych time we agreed, both I and the parishioners (except one or two) that drinkinge should be on the 5 November in remembrance of the deliverance, whych continued for some few years, but after, they desyred to have it on their old day, and so had.

Fifty or so years later another Rector, the Rev. Thomas Ernle, also wrote about the Everley Christmas Ales, which he called 'the riotous custome of Christmasse ale'.

He observes:
> I continued to avoyd the clamours of the ruder sort of the parish, who flock to it as to a Christmasse pastime. I could never learn how this heathenish custome had its first birth or origine, and am sure it is evil report, and noe man can tell into what rudeness in tract of tyme it may degenerate. It were to be wisht it were layd in the dust and utterly forgotten.

In 1755 yet another Rector, Rev. Abraham le Moinse, also attacked the Everley Ales, commenting, 'When I came to this living I found two very bad customs for which no reason can be assigned.'

During his incumbency he changed the date of the Ales to 5 January and also 'altered their style' – though probably temporarily.

To judge from what happened in other parishes in England, though we have no information about the custom at Everley, it could be that the opposition to the Christmas Ales by a succession of rectors, and the determination of the villagers to assert their ancient 'rights', were due to the rector having to provide all the food and drink at his own expense!

In volume 5 of the *Wiltshire Archaeological Magazine* (1852) F. A. Carrington writes:

> I was told in the year 1838, by the late Mr Thomas Neale, of Draycote Foliat, that on Easter Tuesday in every year, the clerk of the adjoining parish of Chiseldon, had an ale; which was effected by the clerk providing a good plain dinner and plenty of strong beer, at his house, for the principal parishioners to partake of; this was called the Clerk's ale, for which each guest made the clerk a present.

He adds a list of gentry who used to attend these ales and 'give their sovereigns and half-sovereigns in return for his good cheer; and I have since been informed that the Clerk's ale at Chiseldon is still kept up, and that it came off as usual on Easter Tuesday, 1854'.

Mr Carrington then gives two Wiltshire instances of what he calls Herd Ales, one at Newnton, the other at Ogbourne St George. He writes, of the Ale at Ogbourne:

The Herd's Ale at Ogbourne St George was described to me by Mrs Charlotte Mills of that place, who is between eighty and ninety years old . . . I will give her statement in her own words:

'Before the enclosure here in 1795, all the people who kept cows at Ogbourne St George used to send them to Roundhill Bottom, which is a place a little further from the village than the two barrows on Swinghill. Humphreys, a cripple, used to keep the cows, and he had a herds' ale every year. He used to have a barrel of beer and victuals, and people used to drink and give him what they chose. I don't know on what day it was, but I know it was when flowers were about, because they made a garland which was put on someone's head, and they danced around it, and they went to gentlemen's houses who used to give them beer. This was when I was about ten years old, and long before the enclosure. There was a large cow common then.'

There is a fuller account of the Herd Ale at Newnton, preserved by John Aubrey and quoted by Mr. Carrington in the above paper. Aubrey writes:

The Parishioners being come to the Dore of the Hayward's house, the Dore was struck thrice in honour of the Holy Trinity, then they entred; the Bell was rung, after which, silence being, their Prayers aforesayd. Then was a Garland of Flowers made upon a hoop brought forth by a Mayd of the Towne upon her Neck; and a young man, (a Batchelour) of another parish first saluted her three times in honour of the holy Trinity, in respect of God the Father. Then she putts the Garland upon his neck, and kisses him 3 times, in honour of the Trinity, particularly God the sonne; Then her putts the Garland on her neck again and kisses her 3 times, and particularly in honour of God the holy ghost. Then he takes the Garland from her neck again by the Custome must give her a penny at least, which (as fancy leades) is now exceeded; as 2s. 6d etc.

The method of giving this Garland is from house to house annually, till it comes round.

In this Evening every Commoner sends his supper up to this house, which is called Eele-howse, and before having layed-in there, equially a stock of Mault, which was brewed in the house, they suppe together, and what was left was given to the Poor.

Aubrey then gives the text of the prayer, which included intercessions for the souls of a number of persons from King Athelstan to an 'abbout' who flourished in the reign of Henry VIII. He also offers an account of the origin of the Ale and its recent history, as follows

King Athelstan having obtained a Victory over the Danes by the assistance of the Inhabitants of this place, riding to recreate himselfe, found a woman bayting of a Cowe upon the waye called the Fosse-way (which is a famous way and runnes through this parish from Cornwall to Scotland). This Woman sate on a stoole, with the Cowe fastened by a rope to the legges of the stoole. The manner of it occasioned the King to ask why she did so? she answered the King, that they had no Common belonging to the towne. The Queen being then in his Company, by their consents it was granted, that the towne should have so much ground in common next adjoyning to this way, as the woman would ride around upon a bare-ridged horse: she undertakes it, and for ascertaining the ground, the King appointed Sir Walter, a Knight that wayted on him, to follow the woman or goe with her; which being donhe, and made known to the Monks at Malmesbury (they to show their Liberality upon the extent of the King's Charity) gave a piece of ground parcell of their Inheritance and adjoyning to the church yard, to build a house upon, for the Hayward to live in, to looke after the Beasts that fed upon this Common. And for to perpetuate the memory of it, appointed the following Prayers to be said upon every Trinity-Sunday, in that house, with the Ceremonie ensueing: and because a Monke of that time, out of his devotion gave a Bell to be rung here at this house before Prayers began, his name was inserted in the Petitions for that gift . . .

In the late warres (i.e. the Civil War of the seventeenth century) this Howse was burnt downe by the Soldiers; and the Custome of Supping is yet (1670) discontinued, together with the brewing that quantity of Drinke. The rest of the Ceremonies are yet continued on the Toft, and on the old dore of the Howse, which yet remains, which they doe then carry thither; and a small quantity of drinke, of 6, or 8 gallons is yet drunke after the Garland is given.

About 1660 one was killed, striving to take-away the Garland.

Another kind of ale, which fell early into disrepute, was the Scot ale, forbidden by edicts of Bishops of Salisbury in 1223 and 1266. 'Scot' is an old English word meaning a payment or levy; it survives in the expression 'scot free'. The 1266 prohibition reads:

We being desirous, for the good of men's souls and bodies, to put down Scot ales and other public drinkings, do, with the consent of our Synod, enjoin all rectors, vicars and other parish priests, in virtue of the obedience which they owe to us, to urge upon their parishioners by frequent exhortations, not to be rash violators of this prohibition.

By *public* drinkings we mean, wherever a multitude of men exceeding the number of ten in the same parish in which the ale shall be sold, or in neighbouring parishes, or within the bounds of the same domicile shall be assembled for the purpose of drinking. But travellers, strangers and persons attending fairs or markets, although they meet in taverns, we are unwilling to include in this prohibition.

6   Local Customs

SOME LOCAL CUSTOMS WERE independent of the calendar. Bull-baiting, for instance, was once widespread in Wiltshire as in other counties, it even being argued that bull beef was neither wholesome nor tasty unless the bull had been baited before slaughter.

Mere is one of the places which preserves recollections of bull-baiting. There was a Bull Ring on Castle Hill, used until early in the nineteenth century. It is remembered that an old woman, Betty Dolby, who was nicknamed 'Bull-riding Betty', used to ride the bulls into the ring.

There are also records of coursing and racing on Mere Down, and the game of fives used to be played by the church tower.

A curfew bell was rung at Mere at eight o'clock in the evening from 18 October to 24 February. The custom was discontinued during the 1914-18 war. Another village with a similar custom, which lasted till the 1960s, is Berwick St John.

About two hundred years ago a rector of the parish, who happened to get lost on the downs one night, left a legacy to perpetuate the ringing of the bell for fifteen minutes every winter night.

The game of cricket was being widely played in Wiltshire early in the nineteenth century. Everley had a tradition that it was one of the first villages in Wiltshire to have a cricket team. In Landford is a field called Wickets' Green which is said to have derived its name from the fact that early cricket matches were played there, before 1834. South Wilts played an All England team in 1854 – and beat them by three runs. This was at Bemerton. Miss Olivier records that cricket was played at Salisbury, Westbury, Stockton, Everley and Pewsey 'in the reign of George III'.

The Winterslow Women's Institute Scrap Book recalls that cricket matches took place on Easton Down in the 1860s, the players then wearing 'box hats'. Pitton, in 1966, revived the memory of a great match played against its neighbour, Farley, for a barrel of beer 'in the field called Howe', a hundred years before. It was possible to fix the date of the match accurately because one of the players, Abram Collins, had to go home during the match because a baby had been born to his wife. The baby, Reuben, died as an old man in the 1930s. It is not recorded which team won the 1866 match, but, if I remember rightly, the centenary event in 1966 was won by Farley. An interesting point about the 1866 match is that it was played in October. In August and September it would have been impossible to get two teams together, almost everyone being engaged in harvest. It would seem, though, that this local Derby came at the end of a cricket season, with matches probably being played regularly in May, June and July, and there is another mention of matches being played in the same field in the 1830s.

An interesting old record describes a 'Bread and Ale' Assize held at Winterslow in 1275. It was presided over by one, John FitzJohn, whose duty it was to check the weight of bread and the consistency of ale – he was, in effect, an early weights-and-measures inspector. A sinister detail, however, was the fact that the Assize was held at 'the Gallows at Winterslow'. These Gallows seem to have been erected by the Roman Road, near the point where the parishes of Winterslow and Winterbourne Dauntsey meet.

Winterslow also had a tradition that parishioners were 'buried with bread and cheese'. Bearers at funerals were always rewarded with bread and cheese and half-a-crown.

Harvest and haymaking existed before schools and had priority over them, in the opinion of village parents. The long school holiday in August and early September was, of course, originally fixed with this in mind. In those hectic weeks it was impossible to get children to school. A quotation from the Log-book of Landford School, taken from the Women's Institute Scrap Book, is typical:—

July 20th, 1868. Children begin to stay away on account of harvest to take their parents' dinner to the field.

I quote this, however, in preference to many similar instances from all over the county because of another entry which follows:

November 2nd, 1868. Am rejoiced to find that Acorning has ended for this Season and that nearly the whole of those absenting themselves on that account have returned to School this morning; having had a most bountiful harvest, such a one as the oldest inhabitants have no recollection.

Presumably the acorns were collected for pig food. At an earlier date they would have been used in bread-making, but not, I think, in the 1860s.

The Landford and Hamptworth Women's Institute Scrap Book also contains an interesting account of cider-making. This is a craft which has died out in most of Wiltshire within living memory. I know of a few cider presses which still operate deep in Somerset but none now within our county boundary. At the turn of the century, however, or just before, there were four cottager-owned cider presses at work in my native village of Pitton alone — and this was a chalkland village, not regarded as good cider-apple country. In those days, however, most farms had a cider-apple orchard, the vestiges of which may still be seen, and many cottagers had a few trees.

The Landford contribution runs:

Until about 1925 cider making was an annual event in this

district. The cider press, an unwieldy and mediaeval-looking contraption, travelled around the country lanes behind a patient horse, and later a less patient lorry, to the orchards and gardens of many of the farmers and cottagers, where it was set up as near to the supply of apples as possible. Often several neighbours would combine to make one operation serve them all.

In spite of the experts who say that only real cider apples should be used, every kind of cooking and dessert apple was pressed, quite literally, into service. Most orchards in those days contained one or two trees of cider apples, beautifully coloured and of most appetising appearance, but which set your teeth on edge if you dared to bite into them.

The first task, once the press and its attendant grinder were installed, was the assembling of every container available in which to catch the precious fluid, and every member of the family was assigned some particular office to fulfil. The grinder, which resembled a giant mincer with a handle on either side, was filled with the fruit, and the cider making had begun.

It took two men to turn the handles to pulp the apples, which were then shovelled into the press between thick felt mats, usually from four to six layers of pulp with inter-leaving mats of each pressing. When this was completed, a huge slab of wood from which protruded a giant screw was lowered on to the sandwich of felt and apple pulp, and every available man, woman and child helped to 'walk it round', like a ship's capstan. The apple juice ran down into a vat beneath, and it was usually the task of the youngest member of the company to watch that this did not overflow.

From this vat the apple juice was transferred to the waiting casks, which were finally moved to their permanent resting places when the day's work was completed. The casks were usually old wine casks, if obtainable those which had held port wine were considered the best, and if a barrel be used more than twice it will take on a woody flavour. Many people added wheat or molasses to help the feeding process, and even meat used to be put in to add to the flavour – a leg of mutton or, best of all, a hambone . . .

This accords very well with what I remember of

cider-making, except that the presses I have seen used mats of straw instead of felt. Iron, sometimes in the form of a horse-shoe, was also at times added to the brew. The cottage cider presses at Pitton were pushed around by hand, as a rule.

The Winterslow Women's Institute Scrap Book mentions several unusual hedgerow crops, including sloes, which were sold to a chemist at West Winterslow. 'The picking was done by families, great boughs being cut and the children sitting all day and picking the berries off into buckets.' Another plant gathered for medicinal purposes was valerian, but this information was taken from a novel by Mrs Arthur Kennard (*Diogeness Sandals*, 1893), who used to come to Winterslow to collect material; and I suspect that in this instance she was referring to some other locality, for valerian is not at all common in the district.

Winterslow was noted for its truffle-hunters. Truffles are an edible underground fungus, of which eight species are to be found in England. They come to maturity in autumn and winter and range in size from a hazel-nut to a tea-cup. The record for England is said to be about two-and-a-half pounds. For centuries they have been prized as delicacies, particularly in Mediterranean countries, where they may still be seen displayed on market stalls.

Until the first world war, truffle-hunting was a recognised autumn and winter occupation for a small group of experts living at Winterslow. The last of them was Alfred Collins, who gave up practising the ancient craft in the 1930s. Eli Collins, his father, was the best known of all the truffle-hunters and a picturesque and notable character, dressed in a velveteen uniform designed and made for him by the contemporary Earl of Radnor. Eli Collins and his truffle-hounds were one of the sights with which the Earl loved to entertain his guests, who marvelled at the skill with which the excited dogs located and disinterred truffles from beneath the great trees of Longford Park.

A hundred years or so ago there were probably ten or a dozen truffle-hunters in Winterslow. In 1860 they sent a petition to Parliament, asking that their dogs should be exempted from the 12 shillings annual tax . . . 'being poor labouring men, living in a woody district of the county where there is a great many English truffles grow, which we cannot find without dogs, we do therefore keep and use a small pudle sort of dog wholly and solely for that and no other ... It has been carried on by our ancestors for generations without paying tax for the dogs.'

One story of the origin of the truffle-hunters is that a Spaniard settled there with his dogs in the reign of Queen Elizabeth I, passing on the secrets of his craft to some of his neighbours. Apart from other considerations, a Spaniard would seem to be an unlikely settler in an English village in Elizabethan times. More probable is the tradition that truffle dogs came to Winterslow from France at some time during the eighteenth century. It is said that they were brought over by a local nobleman, presumably one of the Earls of Holland who then held large estates in the parish. From other estates he had in France, so the story goes, he brought to Winterslow three families of French retainers – the Annetts, the Hatchetts and the LeRoys, which became in translation, King, because the villagers found it difficult to pronounce. Members of all three families still live locally. With them from France came a consignment of the little truffle-hounds. Pictures of some of the dogs survive, and I remember my wife's family once having a dog which was pointed out to me as being 'just like one of them there little truffle-hounds'. It was a lightly built dog, of terrier or poodle type, with a white curly coat.

I suppose that almost any dog could be trained to locate truffles, for the method is straightforward. From puppyhood the dogs are fed on food liberally rubbed with truffle, so that they associate the strong, distinctive scent with food. Then when the dog starts work it is always rewarded with a titbit when it finds a truffle. No doubt, though, the truffle-dogs had a special aptitude for the job. The drawback to training dogs in this country nowadays is obvious. Smearing a dog's meals with imported truffles would be a very costly business.

I am told that it is sometimes possible to locate truffles by lying on the ground under a likely tree on a still autumn afternoon, in such a position that the air just above the ground surface beneath the tree is against a background of clear sky. On such afternoons tiny yellow truffle-flies hatch from ripe truffles and perform their nuptial dance a foot or so above the surface. Dig beneath, and there are likely to be more ripening truffles.

From Winterslow and its neighbourhood, too, I have heard stories of 'colyers'. These are supposed to be ghostly wisps of smoke seen rising on clear days above woods where charcoal-burners once operated. They are, in fact, clouds of midges or gnats, dancing.

Mere had memories of 'squatters'. Edith Olivier, writing in the early 1930s, says: 'Some of the old Squatters' Huts still remain in Mere, although most of them have become derelict.' She quotes the old and widely-held belief that if a man erected a cottage on common land between sunset and sunrise, provided the cottage had a roof, a chimney and a fire lit inside it, he could establish squatters' rights. If in the same time he could put a fence around some of the adjoining land, that became his property too.

The way they managed was to collect, for weeks beforehand, all the material needed, and to hide it in some secret spot. Then they enlisted the sympathy and promise of practical aid of all their friends, and chose a moonlight night for the great undertaking. Split tree-trunks for uprights; rubble, and even brushwood, for filling spaces; clay and mud for the walls and some rough attempt at thatching for the roof – and there you had the hovel . . .

This is how the New Forest village of Nomansland grew up. It lies on the Hampshire-Wiltshire border. A resident, Mrs F. E. Winter, won a county award in a 1946 Women's Institute competition, 'This Was My Village'. She wrote of Nomansland:

Situated on the borders of Hampshire and Wiltshire, and on the edge of the New Forest, it was waste land until about two hundred years ago when some settlers arrived from unknown parts and took possession. It was said that as much land as could be fenced round in twenty-four hours – with a chimney to make a fire – could be had for the taking, and some of the descendants of the original pioneers are still here . . . There are still a few of the early houses left, built of clay and heather trodden into mud, which makes very strong building material. These old houses, when well kept, are very comfortable to live in, as owing to their thick walls and thatched roofs they are warm in winter and cool in summer.

This last remark is certainly true, for I myself lived in a similarly constructed house for about seventeen years.

Many Wiltshire villages have a similar tradition regarding squatters, and many – Winterslow is a good example – have a fairly dense concentration of cottages on land still known as 'The Common'.

In chalkland Wiltshire, however, which comprises the greater part of the county, the building material for such cottages is chalk cob. The following description of building in chalk cob hardly applies to a cottage erected overnight but it is a widely-used traditional method.

The foundation trenches were filled with carefully selected flints, held together by mortar. They were wider than the wall to be erected on top of them and extended above the soil surface by about six inches. Cartloads of rubbly chalk were brought to the site and spread on a levelled plot. Then, donning enormously heavy boots especially made for the purpose or else strengthening their everyday boots by fitting iron soles, two or three of the builders began a kind of clumsy war-dance on the chalk. Meanwhile, some kept the head well dowsed with buckets of water; others threw in more chalk rubble as necessary; others adulterated it with sprinklings of wheat chaff, chopped straw and horse-hair, to give the mixture 'substance' and consistency. After an hour or two, a nice, pasty material had been formed. It stuck like glue to the great boots of the weary 'stampers'. I have heard that there was a Mudwaller's Song, which was chanted during the operation, but I have never met anyone who could remember the words or music.

When the experts felt that the chalk mess was fit for handling, the curious mudwalling prongs were brought into action. I have one of these. It is three-grained, like a Neptune's trident. Each grain is about six inches long, flattened to a width of about an inch, and tapered towards the tip. With these prongs the builders scooped up the gluey chalk and slapped it into position on top of the flints. A layer nine inches to a foot deep was the recognised stint for an evening. That was indeed as much as it was safe to build at one time, before allowing it to set.

When it was set hard, another layer was added, and so the work went on through the warm, cheerful month of May. If we now examine any old wall of chalk cob from which the facing plaster has been removed we can easily discern the layers, or courses, in which the wall was built.

When the walls were finished, they were trimmed off to approximate perpendicularity with a peculiar wooden saw, which was part of the mudwaller's stock in trade. Meantime, the timbers (often salvaged from old wooden ships) were being built into the walls as they were fashioned. The chalk cob dried around them and held them as in a vice. It was a solid house that the mudwallers built.

The interior walls were constructed of wattle-and-daub. Most villagers used to be proficient in hurdle-work, using hazel cut in local woods. The hurdles were reinforced by rough mortar and then plastered over. The funnel-like chimney was built of the same material, except that the upper sections were not plastered over. They were usually left bare and exposed to soot and 'flonkers', and the wonder is that more of them did not catch fire and burn down the house. Yet I have seen many a cottage that has stood for two hundred years or more, the chimneys of which were fashioned in this way.

A high-explosive bomb blew up within twenty yards of such a cottage in 1942. Although newer houses much farther away split and crumbled, the cottage stood intact and unscarred. After the rapid rise in property prices in 1972-73, it changed hands at about £18,000, which must have been at least ten times as much money as the builder had handled in his whole life.

Cob is an ingeniously-conceived material. In districts which lack building stone, it is simply dug from the earth. Provided that its top is protected against rain, a cob wall will last for centuries. When its term of life is eventually over, frost and rain will disintegrate it quickly. Then it can be carted away and spread over the fields from which it was originally dug, to replenish the lime content of the soil. That has been the fate of cob buildings for centuries. The flint foundations are requisitioned for new foundations elsewhere or for road-building. The chalk cob floor can be dug up or ploughed. Soon the very site has been obliterated and forgotten. At Winterslow Ernest Judd (already mentioned on page 67) lived for ninety-nine years in a single-storied cob cottage. He died when the building was burned to the ground. Within a couple of weeks the site was levelled, the garden ploughed up and incorporated in the adjacent field, and no-one would ever have guessed that a building had stood there.

The last chalk cob buildings of which I have any knowledge in Wiltshire were built in the first decade of the present century. During the first world war some of the surviving cob-wallers were pressed into service to instruct soldiers on Salisbury Plain in the ancient craft, in the hope that it might prove useful in trench warfare. Thereafter, neglect and oblivion. I suppose that the last cob-waller has long since died.

Another feature of the chalk country that inherits an ancient tradition is the making of dew-ponds. They are the subject of much talk about mysteries and secret lore. One dew-pond maker, advertising in the 1930s, used to refer to a 'secret process having been handed down from father to son for over 250 years'.

Often the ponds seem to be associated with prehistoric earthworks, and this has earned them the reputation of great antiquity. One reads references to 'neolithic dew-ponds' but there is no real justification for this. Earthworks and dew-ponds are found on the crests of chalk hills for different reasons, and, although the prehistoric inhabitants of the hill forts may well have obtained their water supply from similar ponds, there is little likelihood that any existing ponds have their origin so far back.

The only one for which genuine antiquity may perhaps be claimed is on Milk Hill, overlooking the Vale of Pewsey. A Saxon survey dated AD 825 refers to a hill pond named 'Oxenmere' on the boundary of Alton Priors, and there today is the dew pond, still marking the boundary of the parish of Alton Priors. Therefore, one is tempted to conclude, it has been there ever since.

That is possible, but only if the pond has been kept clean and had its lining restored regularly over the period of 1,150 years. The average age of a dew-pond would seem to be not more than 100-150 years. 'Oxenmere' has probably been remade many times. At Maiden Castle, in Dorset, for example, there is a dew-pond which would seem to be genuinely prehistoric and connected with the town which the Romans sacked, but there is definite evidence that it was constructed within the past hundred years or so.

The other myth concerning dew-ponds is that they are fed by dew. It *is* a myth. Experiments have shown that the greatest deposit of dew, using the most favourable collecting surface and best possible weather, amounts to .0024 inches in a night. If every night of the year were equally favourable, the optimum collection would be .876 inches a year, but the actual total would probably be less than half that amount.

The explanation of the replenishment of the ponds is perfectly simple. They are fed by rainwater. Most of them occur in areas with a rainfall of between 27 and 40 inches, which, with an evaporation rate of 18 inches a year, leaves a fair surplus. However, the ponds do better than that. Each is surrounded by a catchment area much greater than the surface area of the water.

A simple calculation will show how important this catchment area is. If we have a pond 20 yards square its surface area is 400 square yards. If it is surrounded by a margin equal in width to the radius of the pond, the catchment area is increased to 1,600 square yards.

An inch of rain represents a fall of approximately 22,500 gallons per acre. On a pond of 400 square yards that would amount to 1,866 gallons. A 30-inch annual rainfall would thus feed the pond with 54,980 gallons, from surface catchment alone. But the total catchment area, allowing for the sloping margin around the pond, is four times as great. The total annual replenishment is thus 219,920 gallons. An 18-inch annual evaporation rate accounts for 33,588 gallons. The surplus is thus 186,332 gallons. Even allowing for, say, half the water that falls on the catchment margin being lost through wastage, the surplus is still substantial.

Allowance must of course be made for the fact that the maximum rate of evaporation and of water use by animals coincides with what is often the period of lowest rainfall, namely, high summer. Otherwise the hill-top ponds would never dry up, and sometimes they do.

If the explanation of the 'dew-pond' is thus so straightforward and scientific, wherein lies the 'secret' of the traditional pond-makers? The answer is, partly in a thorough appreciation of the importance of the catchment margin and partly in the methods of making the bottom of the pond waterproof. There can be no doubt that a good deal of traditional skill and ingenuity went into the pond's construction. A favourite bottom layer was composed of puddled chalk, treated to form much the same substance as the chalk cob we have just been discussing. Other experts used clay, sometimes mixed with lime. The lowest layer was generally covered by a stratum of straw, laid in the form of thatch, though some practitioners have held that straw is not necessary. The top layer is of a variety of loose materials, such as sand, gravel, flint and chalk rubble.

Towards the end of its normal life of 100 to 150 years, a pond will probably have silted up sufficiently to have necessitated its cleaning out several times, and each cleaning will probably have pared a little off the bottom. It then needs to be remade. Sheep may well help to keep a pond waterproof by consolidating the bottom with their hoofs, but heavier animals tend to wear it into holes.

The Winterslow Scrap Book records that 'there were many dew ponds and about 20 wells . . . The dew-ponds supplied the needs of the farm animals . . . and, it has been said, beer was brewed from dew-pond water.' This would not surprise me. Perhaps the pond at the Pheasant Inn, originally called the 'Winterslow Hutt', was once used in this way. A contributor to the Winterslow Scrap Book remembers: 'At this horse pond the steam traction engines used to refill after they had been steamed dry by the Three Mile Hill out of Salisbury. They were just able to run down the hill from The Haven'.

Familiarity with these ponds gives point to a favourite story told by dialect comedians at village concerts not many years ago. It concerns a farmer's wife who scolded an itinerant traction engine driver for filling his engine with water from the farm pond. After a lively exchange, in which she found she was by no means getting the better of the argument, she conceded, 'Oh well, I suppose you'd better have it. But take the water out of the middle of the pond, Our cows drink round the outside!'

One of the great dew-pond makers of Wiltshire was Tom Smith, Market Lavington, who was active as late as the 1930s.

Another notable rural craftsman from the same district was Mr Lancaster, of Great Cheverell, who specialised in sheep bells. Some shepherds made do with old tins, with an iron bolt serving as a clapper, but Lancaster's bells were works of art. I possess several. They are made from sheets of some metal alloy, which evidently includes brass, and are beautifully shaped. They are fastened by leather thongs, cut from old harness, to wooden yokes.

These yokes, too, show great craftsmanship, carved by the shepherds themselves during their leisure summer weeks while the sheep were grazing on the downs. They were generally of gorse wood, which contained a natural angle, and were carved with a pocket knife, which was also used for cutting bread and cheese and for paring sheep's hooves. The leather thongs were passed through two slots in the yokes and fastened in place by pins. The pins, arrow-shaped, are likewise exquisitely carved. W. E. Wright, of Harnham, who used to collect such items, once showed me a wand of yew wood, three feet long, shaped into bell pegs. The shepherd snapped one off when he needed it. The patience needed to carve these pegs, in dry yew wood with only a pocket knife for a tool, must have been considerable. In my collection I have another peg cut from sheep's bone.

The bells were used primarily in summer, when the sheep grazed over wide areas of unfenced down. The shepherd possessed perhaps a dozen bells, which he fastened to the necks of the leaders of the flock, generally old ewes, who had been about for a few years and were decidedly cunning if not wise. Where they went, the other sheep would follow. The shepherd could then settle down for the day, whittling away more bell yokes or other objects, confident in the knowledge that the bells would tell him just where the sheep were and what they were doing.

As a sheep grazes it moves for a step or two and then pauses. So when the shepherd heard, as he hoped to do for hour after hour, a gentle, desultory tinkling he knew that all was well. Sometimes this would be interrupted by a rhythmical swinging of several bells, indicating that the sheep were on the march, perhaps to the nearest pond for a drink or perhaps to some prohibited place. It then was worth the shepherd's while to check on them. Sometimes he would hear a wild jangling – an alarm call. The sheep were startled, by a fox or a dog perhaps. The shepherd dropped his work quickly and went to find out what was happening.

An old Wiltshire proverb says that a good cowman should be 'one-legged and dumb', meaning that he could neither chase the cows nor shout at them. A shepherd might operate with the same handicaps, provided he had a good dog, but he could never afford to be deaf.

Bells from my collection were last used on the necks of sheep in 1963 or 1964. Having been caught napping once or twice by a particularly obstreperous and artful ram named Oscar, I fitted him with a bell, so that I would know just where he was when I was inspecting the flock.

I also have a shepherd's throwing-stick, carved for me, from memory, not many years ago by my brother-in-law, Harold Pearce. It is about two feet long, and heavier at one end than at the other. The shepherd would have used it for throwing at rabbits sitting in a 'squat' in a hedge, or at birds, and would have been quite accurate with it. Quite possibly sticks like these were the cudgels used in fighting single combats at fairs and other events. During the second half of the nineteenth century some shepherds used to carve their throwing-sticks in low relief and sell them as souvenirs at autumn fairs. One I have seen was carved with objects that had caught the shepherd's fancy – his knife, his crook, his kettle and a passing pheasant. Another depicted a fox hunt.

Shepherds' crooks which I have used, and indeed all those I have seen in Wiltshire, have been leg-crooks – that is, they were made for catching a sheep by the hind leg. The crooks themselves were blacksmith-made, of iron. I have heard, however, that in the parts of Cranborne Chase which lie in Wiltshire neck crooks were sometimes used, the crook in one instance being made of deer's horn.

Curious customs which have completely disappeared, though apparently once widely practised, are skimmetting and smock weddings.

'Skimmetting', also called 'rough music', was a communal attempt to shame a wife-beater, or, occasionally, an adulterer. My father could just remember a skimmetting which took place at Pitton when he was a small boy, in the early 1880s. A large party of villagers, armed with tin trays, drums and anything else that made a noise, assembled outside the man's house. There for about an hour they jeered, shouted abuse at him, and made as much racket as possible. They came well provided with lumps of cowdung, rotten eggs, buckets full of slops and other unpleasant objects, which they hoped to throw at him if he showed his face, but he did not, so they contented themselves with throwing their missiles at the door and windows. It must have been an effective demonstration. My father could not remember what crime the man had committed but thought it had been a flagrant affair with another man's wife.

Earlier accounts of the custom make a distinction between Skimmetting, which was applied to wife-beaters and, it appears, hen-pecked husbands, and the 'Hoosit Hunt' a penalty for immorality. Details of the two, and the difference between them, were recorded and summarised in an article 'Moonrake Medley', which appeared in the *Wiltshire Archaeological Magazine,* Vol. 50 (1943):

A paper by F. A. Carrington, of Ogbourne St George, on certain ancient Wiltshire customs appeared in our very first number, just ninety years ago, and one of the customs described is the 'Wooset'. [The 'W' is silent]. Carrington had seen two – one at Burbage in 1835, and the other at Ogbourne St George about 1840. From his description they seemed to lack little or nothing of their earlier elaboration, the processions taking place on nine nights out of a consecutive fifteen. Both, it should be noted, dealt with cases of conjugal infidelity. The Skimmington was reserved for henpecked husbands. The two processions, he says, were different. The rough band of frying-pans, old kettles filled with stones, sheep's horns, cracked sheep-bells, discarded fish-kettle beaten with a marrowbone, or any other instrument, we may suppose, supplied by the village dump, doubtless figured in both, but in place of the seven-foot cross carrying a chemise on its arms and on its head a horse's skull with a pair of deer horns attached, which formed the main exhibit of the 'Ooset', the principal group in the Skimmington was the stuffed figure of a man placed on horseback with a man in woman's clothes riding behind him and beating the figure about the head with a wooden ladle . . .

Two personal accounts of Oosit Hunts, by a Mr E. R. Pole, were then given:

Mr Richard Hill, of Ramsbury, now residing at Crofton, remembers clearly that when a lad of about ten years old he saw 'Oosit hunting' at Ramsbury in the year 1868 or 1869.

A man known to have been unfaithful to his wife, although they had a large family (and for that reason the name is withheld), was the object.

A procession was formed led by a man holding the skeleton of a horse's head on a stick, its jaws made to open and shut by pulling a string, with a rough band consisting of trumpets, trombones, kettle-drums, etc., followed by a rabble with pots and pans and anything they could make a noise on or with. They paraded up to and around the man's house for three or four nights, each night the crowd increasing. The police tried to stop them but were unable to do so.

And here is the second instance:

Returning from Bedwyn station on the afternoon of the 17th April, 1943, I was walking down the village street when I met an old inhabitant now living at Stokke Common and stopped to speak to him. His age is eighty-four.

'Well, how are you? You are just the chap I want to ask a question of. What do you know of 'Osit-hunting'?'

'You don't mean Osit-hunting. It is Oosit-hunting. Do you want a horse's head? You know – a skeleton? I know where there is one which I can get you,' he said, with a gleam in his eye.

'No, I don't want to do any hunting, but weren't you active in an Oosit-hunt in 1895.'

'Yes,' he laughed, 'Mr. X and Miss Y of Little Bedwyn.'

'That's it,' I said. 'Now what did you do?'

'Well, there was old so-and-so and several others (whom he named) and myself, we were all in it, but I don't think that time we could get hold of a horse's head, but for three nights we went to both houses – a large number of us – with a rough band. You know – pots and pans and kettles and anything we could make a noise on, and we did give it 'em!'

'Was that the last one you remember around here?'

'Well, there was another at Shalbourne about the same time, but I can't remember now if it was before this Bedwyn one or not. I think it was a few months after.'

Of course Mr X. was a married man with children, and Miss Y needs no comment.

Smock weddings belong to an earlier age. It used to be generally believed that if a man married a widow other than by a smock wedding he took over the debts of her former husband. To avoid this, she came to him naked, thus demonstrating that she brought nothing with her from her previous life. Decency had to be preserved, however, so she came to church dressed in a sheet or a smock, purchased by the bridegroom. The latest Wiltshire example which I have been able to find occurred at Chitterne All Saints on 17 October 1714. The parish register states that on that day: 'John Bridmore and Anne Selwood were married, the aforesaid Anne Selwood was married in her smock, without any clothes or headgier on.'

7 Wiltshire Characters and Personalities

PROFESSOR CHARLES THOMAS, excavating near Everley in 1953, was told that Ludgershall, about five miles away, took its name from King Lud who had lived in the castle there. It is true that the town has the remains of a medieval fortress. He also heard of an immense chain of caves, supposed to lead from a farm near Ludgershall under Sidbury Hill and on from there to near Pewsey, where there was another entrance - a total distance of almost ten miles. On investigation, caves were found to exist but proved neither particularly significant nor extensive. They are near Longbottom Farm.

As to King Lud, his name is identical with the mythical ancient British figure, reputed to have founded London in pre-Roman times. But Ludgershall, so far as early records show, appears to incorporate an Old English name, Lutgar. Ludgate Hill, popularly believed to commemorate the Lud of

London more likely derives from the gate which stood there, since Old English *ludgeat* means back gate. Between Tudor times and the dismantling of the gate in 1760, a statue of King Lud stood on the site, and he was therefore no doubt a well-known figure. Hence, most likely, the association of his name with Ludgershall.

One of Professor Thomas' informants was an old gardener, born in Everley in about 1880, who had many legends and traditions, 'handed down to me from my grandfather'. One of these concerned King Ina, the remains of whose castle he drew attention to, at the foot of Sidbury Hill. In fact there are some old earthworks near the hill, and King Ina is associated with the area. He was King of Wessex from 688-726 and is supposed to have fought the Mercians at Adam's Grave, a few miles north-west of Sidbury, in 715.

Adam's Grave, actually a barrow, is mentioned in records of 110 years later under the name Wodnesbeorge – Woden's Barrow. The county possesses a number of names connected with Woden, almost certainly dating from the period, probably less than a century in duration, between the arrival of the Saxons and their conversion to Christianity. This began in 634. The most famous is the Wansdyke, an earthwork above the Vale of Pewsey, which we first know of as Wodnes dic (903). The actual history of both the Barrow and the Dyke was presumably forgotten before they were nominally provided with a supernatural origin, probably during the latter half of the 6th century. This is particularly interesting in the case of the Wansdyke, know to be post-Roman and therefore not particularly old at the time, yet surely a memorable construction. It seems that, retentive though the folk memory sometimes is, in other circumstances it is surprisingly forgetful.

Like Ina, King Alfred the Great was of course a historical personality, though his association with some parts of Wiltshire is purely legendary. He was known south of Warminster as 'him of Stourton', this certainly until the turn of the century. The reference is to the south-westernmost parish in the county, though the tower named after him, marking the spot where he supposedly raised his standard against the Danes, lies just beyond the county boundary, in Somerset. But Brixton Deverill, where local legend places the mishap with the cakes is six miles north-east of Stourton, well within Wiltshire. Brixton Deverill rectory, so the villagers used to claim, stands just north of the spot where the cakes were burned – presumably in the late 870s.

Another early hero of Wiltshire, John Rattlebone, has two memorials in Sherston. One is the name of the local inn, the Rattlebone; the other, a little carved figure near the south door of the church, is alleged to be his likeness, but this is improbable.

Rattlebone is supposed to have been involved in a great fight between the Saxons and the Danes in 1016. Sceorstan, which ancient documents give as the site of the battle, is said to be Sherston. Although inconclusive, it was a fierce contest and Rattlebone received a terrible wound in the stomach. His bowels began spilling out, but he seized a tile and held it against the wound to hold them in while he fought on. Evidently he survived, for he was given the manor of Sherston as a reward for his valour. The village has an old song which runs:

> Fight well, Rattlebone;
> Thou shalt have Sherston.

In the church there is a massive timber chest, dating from the Middle Ages. It was used to store Rattlebone's armour according to a local tradition. The initials 'R.B.' are carved upon it.

Wishford church in the south of the county commemorates another knight, Sir Thomas Bonham, who lived there in the fifteenth century. Bonham had a familiar problem – increasing commitments and a static income. He already had too many dependents when his wife gave birth to twins. The story goes that, as a desperate attempt at birth control, he said goodbye to his wife and went off to foreign wars.

When he returned at the end of seven years Bonham was at first unrecognised, for he was wearing pilgrim's clothes and had not shaved since leaving Wiltshire. However, he showed a ring which established his identity. His wife acknowledged him and next year gave birth to seven children all at once. It seems he would have done as well to stay at home.

The babies were carried to Wishford church in a sieve to be baptised, and afterwards it hung there for many years. In 1828 three old villagers remembered seeing it when they were children, and the Oak Apple Day procession used to include seven dolls carried in a sieve. Wishford church contains an effigy of Sir Thomas dressed in pilgrim's clothing, together with his large family, though some of the children are missing.

One version of the tale includes a witch. It seems that Lady Bonham had given up all hope of ever seeing her husband again and was about to marry another man. But a local witch travelled by magic means to the distant land where Sir Thomas was living and brought him home. The Bonham memorial in Wishford church has a small female figure perched on a stone by Sir Thomas' head, and people say that this is the witch.

Similar stories are told of other places. There is one attached to Upton Scudamore, near the source of the Wylye river, though I suppose that, in this instance, the tale may have travelled upstream from Wishford.

William Darrell, the 'Wild' Darrell of legend, was a less attractive nobleman. He lived in Littlecote House, near Chilton Foliat. One dark and stormy night in 1575 Mother Barnes, a Shefford midwife, was summoned to a confinement. The payment was very generous but she was blindfolded and taken, riding pillion on horseback, seven or eight miles across the downs to a fine manor house.

In due course she delivered the baby and asked Darrell for some clothes in which to dress it. He told her to throw the child on the fire. Appalled, she begged him to let her keep it for herself, but he pushed her aside, seized the baby and threw it into the flames. She was then blindfolded, led downstairs and taken home.

Next morning she went to a magistrate and told him her story. Fortunately she had snipped a piece off the bed-cover and had counted the number of stairs. Darrell was suspected and in due course Mother Barnes was able to identify Littlecote House as the place she had visited. Darrell was arrested and brought to trial. The jury acquitted him. A few months later he was thrown from his horse, at a place still called Darrell's Stile, and broke his neck.

The events have given rise to various ghost stories. It is said that Darrell's horse shied at the apparition of the murdered child, that his ghost still walks by Darrell's Stile, and that Littlecote House is haunted, though by a chill sense of evil rather than by any identifiable apparition.

Local tradition held that Darrell was acquitted through the influence of the Attorney General at that time, who happened to be a distant cousin of his. That sounds likely enough. It has also been suggested that the mother of the baby was Darrell's sister and that he was guilty of incest.

On Darrell's death the estate passed to Sir John Popham, who was judge at the trial. That too is suggestive, and Sir Walter Scott, in the story he wove around the events, makes Sir John receive the estate as a bribe. It does not match what is known of Sir John's character, but the whole tragedy is obscure.

Some of the stories attached to Dick Turpin really belong to a Wiltshire highwayman, Thomas Boulter. Black Bess was actually the name of Boulter's horse. He stole her from Erlestoke Park one night, and she carried him for years. Mounted presumably on Black Bess, he rode eighty miles from Windsor to his home at Poulshot. Usually he changed horses at intervals on a long journey, as highwaymen did, but on this occasion he rode the same animal all the way. He had held up three coaches between Windsor and Maidenhead and was closely pursued.

Born in 1748, he was the son of the miller at Poulshot. He worked at his father's mill until he was twenty-six years old and then moved to the Isle of Wight, where he started a milliner's shop. Finding that he was losing more money than he was making, he became a highwayman.

He started on the Great West Road, holding up a coach between Stockbridge and Salisbury. We know much about his career and what his feelings were, because, in the condemned cell, he was granted a three-weeks' reprieve to write his memoirs, or confessions. He seems to have been a sensitive, indeed timid, man, who was always polite to his victims. Apparently he never hurt anyone. In Wiltshire he was popularly known as 'a gentleman of the road', and many tales were told about him.

On one occasion he escaped from prison by cutting a hole in the prison wall. He rode from Blandford via Weymouth and Honiton to Exeter, having seized £500. Arrested and sentenced to death, he was reprieved on condition that he joined the army, but his military service lasted just four days before he absconded.

Although his financial difficulties soon disappeared, the

excitement of his new way of life made it impossible for him to return to the dull business of shop-keeping. Maybe family influence had something to do with it, for his father, the miller, had once been whipped in Devizes Market-Place for robbing an old women, and his brother had been a highwayman, too, until crippled in a hold-up. At last Thomas's luck ran out. He was betrayed at Bridport and was hanged at Winchester on August 19th, 1778.

Boulter was one of a succession of notorious Wiltshire highwaymen. Three of the most celebrated were operating in the last two decades of the seventeenth century. James Whitney was a son of the manse. His father, the former rector of Donhead St. Andrew, had been evicted under the Commonwealth for Royalist sympathies. Whitney was more ruthless than Boulter. He formed a gang strong enough to fight pitched battles with any victims who resisted, as happened when they held up the Oxford stage-coach. On one occasion the gang got away with £15,000, which, allowing for the difference in currency values, must have been nearly on a par with the Great Train Robbery. Eventually they were captured by a troop of dragoon guards and hanged at Smithfield.

Biss was another highwayman from a well-to-do family. He was said to be the son of the vicar of Bishopstrow, whose family owned property at Upton Scudamore and Tisbury. He had the reputation of being a Robin Hood, robbing the rich but helping the poor. His end was predictable. He was hanged at Salisbury in 1695.

William Davis, yet another highwayman, was hanged at Tyburn in 1689. He was not a Wiltshireman but conducted most of his operations on Salisbury Plain. Like the other 'gentlemen highwaymen' he was reasonably prosperous and owned a farm and an inn. His career apparently lasted nearly forty years – unusually long for such a hazardous profession.

On the other side of Devizes, by the Salisbury road on the edge of the downs, beyond West Lavington, stands a memorial stone, often hidden in long grass, with an interesting inscription. It is on the Devizes side of the junction with the by-road to the abandoned village of Imber, and the wording runs:

At this spot Mr Dean of Imber was attacked and robbed by

four highwaymen in the evening of October 21, 1839. After a spirited pursuit of three hours, one of the Felons, Benjamin Colclough, fell dead on Chittern Down. Thos Saunders, George Waters and Richard Harris were eventually captured, and were convicted at the ensuing Quarter Sessions at Devizes, and transported for a term of fifteen years. This monument is erected by public subscription as a warning to those who presumptuously think to escape the punishment God has threatened against Thieves and Robbers.

I have heard, from a source which I have forgotten, a vivid elaboration of this story. On being held up by the four highwaymen, Farmer Dean proposed a wager.

'I'll bet,' he said, 'that I'm a better shot than any of you lot.'

'Look,' he said, 'We'll throw my hat in the air, and the one who puts most holes in it before it touches the ground takes the money.'

They agreed, and the firing began.

'Wait a bit,' said one of the highwaymen, after a time, as he retrieved the much-battered hat. 'The pistols are empty.'

'Mine isn't!' said Farmer Dean. 'Hands up!'

The story of the subsequent chase reveals one interesting fact. It would appear that, contrary to the popular image of highwaymen as cavalier-type gentlemen on horseback, these robbers were on foot. Their names and behaviour would indicate local men, engaged in felony as a sideline.

Wiltshire had its own lady highwayman, whose career, as it happened, was very short. Mary Sandall was a Baverstock women, aged twenty-four. She apparently went out on the road from a sense of adventure, since she could afford a good horse and her hauls were trifling. Armed with a pistol and dressed as a man, she held up a neighbour, a Mrs Thring of Burcombe, and robbed her of two shillings and a black silk cloak. The alarm was raised, and Mary was soon caught. She was tried, sentenced to death but reprieved, and there her story ends.

Another monument to the retribution which our ancestors thought, or hoped, would fall on the unrighteous can be seen in Devizes Market-place. Its central position and imposing appearance show what an impression the incident which it describes made on the town's eighteenth-century citizens. The monument itself is quite large and impressive. The inscription reads:

> On Thursday the 25th January, 1753, Ruth Pierce of Pottern in this county, agreed with three other women to buy a sack of wheat in the market, each paying her due proportion towards the same. One of these women, in collecting the several quotas of money, discovered a deficiency and demanded of Ruth Pierce the sum which was wanting to make good the amount. Ruth Pierce protested that she had paid her share, and said that she wished she might drop down dead if she had not. She rashly repeated this wish; when, to the consternation and terror of the surrounding multitude, she instantly fell down and expired, having the money concealed in her hand.

Two other 'ladies of the road' are remembered for much more pedestrian careers. Salisbury Museum contains prints of Mrs Rideout and the Coombe Express – which enjoyed quite a vogue towards the end of last century. She was an old market-women in bonnet and shawl, who used to bring produce to Salisbury Market in a little cart drawn by donkeys, popularly known as 'The Coombe Express'. Her Salisbury depot was the Shoulder of Mutton inn, in Bridge Street.

It is interesting that the downland track from Salisbury to Coombe Bissett and on to Whitsbury used to be marked by what were known as 'chalk lights'. These were little heaps of chalk, about a foot high, arranged alongside the broad, grassy track at regular intervals. As the carrier's cart drew abreast of one 'light' on a winter evening the next would be seen with the help of the oil or candle carriage lamps. This prevented the cart from straying off course over the open downs.

The other lady who should be commemorated for her industry was Eliza Harding. In her little book *Moonrakings*, Edith Olivier writes: 'When the drovers came down the lane with the sheep she would have ready outside her house (at Netton) a small table with cakes and bread and cheese, and by the side a cask of ale, so that the drovers could stop and partake of light refreshments, also to exchange news, for it was not necessary at that time to have a licence to sell ale'. She was, in fact, the forerunner of the modern roadhouse.

Maud Heath was another market-women who lived in the fifteenth century at Langley Burrell. Every market day she trudged into Chippenham Market with baskets of eggs and poultry, seldom failing to get her feet soaked when struggling through the marshy ground beside the Avon. When she died she left her life's savings to construct a path so that future generations could walk to Chippenham Market dry-footed. Maud Heath's Causeway is still there, a pleasant afternoon's walk in summer. It is four miles long and at one end an inscription in stone records:

From this Wick Hill begins the praise
Of Maud Heath's gifts to those highways.
At the other end a matching tablet declares:
Hither extendeth Maud Heath's gift
For where I stand is Chippenham Clift.

And on a hill overlooking the Causeway sits a stone effigy of Maud Heath herself, with her stick and basket of eggs. Beneath it, yet another inscription effuses:

Thou who dost pause on this aerial height
Where Maud Heath's Pathway winds in shade or light
Christian wayfarer in a world of strife
Be still and ponder on the Path of Life.

W.L.B.

W.L.B., the Rev. William L. Bowles, was vicar of Bremhill in 1838; together with the Marquis of Lansdowne, the lord of the manor, he erected the monument.

At Purton according to tradition, there is another example of feminine initiative. The church has two towers, the central one surmounted by a spire. Purton people say that this unusual architecture resulted from a quarrel between two sisters who were paying for the building. One wanted a spire, the other a tower, so the church was given both. Unfortunately for the story, the western tower was added about 150 years after the spire, which was built in 1325.

A legend relates that when the Bishop of Salisbury decided to move his cathedral from the bleak hill-top site at Old Sarum down to the pleasanter meadows by the Avon, an archer stood on the ramparts of Old Sarum and shot an arrow in approximately the right direction. Where it fell, the new cathedral was built.

It seems a strange story, for the direct distance from Old Sarum to Salisbury cathedral is only just short of two miles. I doubt if even the most proficient mediaeval longbowman was as good as that.

Whatever the legend of its siting, the new building's architecture was to inspire a certain Daniel Rogers, native of Salisbury, to write as follows:

> As many days as in one year there be,
> So many windows in this church you see
> As many marble pillars here appear
> As there are hours through the fleeting year.
> As many gates as moons one here does view;
> Strange tale to tell, yet not more strange than true.

Possibly the tale of the Old Sarum archer inspired a rather similar story, of much more recent date, which is told of Swindon. It is said that in 1840 the great engineer, Isambard Kingdom Brunel, and a colleague, Daniel Gooch, when surveying possible routes for the Great Western Railway, sat to have a picnic on a plot of rough, gorse-studded ground near the little market town of Swindon. When the meal was finished Brunel threw a sandwich and remarked, 'That's where we'll build'. And that is where the first buildings of the railway's great complex at Swindon were in due course erected.

Long after Old Sarum ceased to be inhabited it remained a borough and sent two members to Parliament. It was, in fact, held up as a most glaring example of a 'rotten borough' in the debate preceding the passing of the Reform Act in 1832. A directory of the 1860s says:

> A tree, near Stratford, was the place of nominal election for the borough of Old Sarum, but, almost immediately after the Reform Bill, a violent wind blew down the principal part of the tree; its decaying stump is still much visited by the curious; several large areas of it were broken down and carried off as trophies by the exulting populace, when the passing of the Reform Bill disenfranchised the borough.

Later the spot was marked by a sarsen boulder with a suitable inscription. The field in which it stands is called 'Election Acre'.

On a hill commanding a distant view of Salisbury spire, two miles away to the west, stood Clarendon Palace, one of Wiltshire's most interesting mediaeval sites. The date of its origin is unknown, but it was there before the cathedral was built. It flourished throughout the Middle Ages and was at one time reputed to be the second largest building in England. Monarch after monarch lavished care and money upon Clarendon, which was a favourite royal hunting centre in times of peace. In an age of austere castles it lacked the normal fortifications and exhibited many features of the later manor houses. Excavations in the 1930s produced evidence of much lavish decoration, including splendid wall paintings and glazed tiles made on or near the site.

Apart from kings, the historical character most closely associated with Clarendon is St Thomas à Becket, who in his early years as a parish priest at Winterbourne Earls used to walk over to Clarendon to conduct mass. The path he followed was, within living memory, known as St Thomas' Path and was supposed to be always green, even in winter.

Mounted knights riding along the Roman road from Winchester would turn off for Clarendon at a point due east of the Palace, not far from the village of Pitton. They would travel for the last mile or two along the crest of a hill known locally as Joyners Hill, and Pitton has a legend of ghostly horsemen seen from time to time riding along this route.

To Broad Hinton belongs the legend of the handless knight. The church there contains a memorial to a character who lived in the sixteenth century, the knight Sir Thomas Wroughton. He and his four children are all portrayed without hands. The legend is that, coming home hungry from a day's hunting, Sir Thomas found his wife Anne reading the Bible instead of cooking his dinner. He angrily seized the book and threw it in the fire. Anne managed to rescue it but badly burnt her hands. Thereafter the hands of Sir Thomas and his four children withered.

Sir Thomas Wroughton's experience showed in the clearest terms the contempt for fleshly pleasures in his time. Edward Slow, the Wilton dialect poet, made a similar point, though less directly, nearly four centuries later. Here is his poem of

1903 in phonetic dialect, on *The Leabourer's Zundy Marnin*. The labourer has been to church:

> The marnin zarvice now is o'er,
> Wie zolemn step a laves the door;
> Wie childern, seeks agean his cot,
> An thinks how happy is his lot;
> While busy wife da quick prepare
> The Sabbath meal of humble fare;
> A piece of bwiled beakon hot,
> An vegetables vrim gierden plot;
> An zuety dumplins, roun an plump,
> Which meaks the hager chidern jump,
> Ta tha leabourer tis indeed a treat
> That he zich vare as this can greet;
> Var on wirken days out in the the viel
> On brade an cheese he makes his meal.
> An who shall say these voke be zinners
> Ta zit down to cook'd Zundy dinners . . .

The last two lines indicate that the poor still had guilty feelings about enjoying such luxuries.

Slow enjoyed a considerable vogue in his day; his verses were often recited at village concerts and similar functions. I have heard, in the 1920s and 1930s, more renderings of *The Gurt Big Viggetty Pudden* than I care to remember.

David Saunders, 'the Shepherd of Salisbury Plain', died over a century before Slow's description of the Sunday dinner. Simple fare, some might now say, though filling and good. Times were harder in David's day.

In the nineteenth century the tracts by the Somerset philanthropist, Hannah More, enjoyed a wide popularity, none more than the one about this shepherd. David lived at Littleton, near Lavington, in extreme poverty. He, his wife and sixteen children occupied a hovel consisting of one room upstairs and one below. His rustic philosophy, based on regular reading of the big Bible which he kept under the thatch of his cottage, and his saintly acceptance of the hardships of life, strongly commended him to the reading public of those days – consisting, naturally, of people who were considerably better off. He died in 1796, but the book of his life was still in circulation in the 1870s.

Here is David Saunders writing just after the middle of the eighteenth century:

> Our little maids, before they are six years old, can first get a halfpenny, and then a penny a day, by knitting. The boys are too little to do hard work, but get a trifle by keeping the birds off the corn; for this the farmer will give them a penny or twopence, and now and then a bit of bread and cheese into the bargain. When the season of crow-keeping is over, then they glean or pick stones; anything is better than idleness, and if they did not get a farthing by it, I would make them do it just the same, for the sake of giving them early habits of labour.

The children also collected wool from the brambles, and Mrs. Saunders used this to knit them stockings. She was confined to bed with rheumatism, and half-a-crown given to David was spent on brown sugar and ale to add to the water-gruel on which she was living.

8 Witches, Giants and the Devil

A WILTSHIRE LADY, more notorious than celebrated, was Lyddie Shears, the Winterslow witch, who lived in the first half of the nineteenth century. The Scrap Book of the Winterslow Women's Institute records the main facts of her life and reputation:

> Even at the beginning of this century tales of Lydia Shears used to be bandied about the markets, Romsey Market in particular. It is said that she used to offer gypsy merchandise at the doors of the cottages, and that those who had the moral courage to refuse would be free of her evil influence, but that those who had not, did her bidding . . .
>
> An old man told Mr Collins that in his young poaching days, if they took Lyddie backy and snuff, she would go out

with flint and steel striking sparks which attracted hares so that the poachers could knock them over. The legend is that she so teased a certain Farmer Tanner by turning herself into a hare for him to course with his greyhounds, the hare always disappearing in her garden, that the farmer sought the advice of the Rector of Tytherley. The good man recommended that a bullet be made of a sixpenny-piece. The farmer with it shot the elusive hare, and the witch was found dead in her cottage with a silver bullet in her heart!

Edith Olivier was able to provide a few additional details. Her version of the final episode runs: 'The hare was shot dead as it entered the garden. But afterwards, as they called at the cottage, they saw the body of Lydia Shears lying on the floor dead, and upon examination the silver bullet was found to have caused her death.' This was a traditional method of killing a witch (in animal form or otherwise).

There is ample room for speculation here. Murder? Sleight of hand? Coincidence? Shock? An earlier legend attaching to a nineteenth-century character? There is also the fact that similar stories, including the detail about the silver bullet, are told in different parts of England.

Moonrakings mentions a witch of Wootton Rivers 'who lived at Goblin's Hold and whose face was seen at her window by many people long after she was said to be dead'. It also records the instance of a man bewitched in 1922, by two South Wiltshire wizards; the spell was eventually broken by another witch. The two wizards are said to have been named Cobley and Brewster, and the benevolent witch was a Mrs. Williams, but the locality is not recorded as some of the people involved were still alive when the book was written.

For the same reason I shall not name places or people, but I do know of more than one alleged witch in Wiltshire today, and they are regarded with superstitious anxiety by their neighbours.

Salisbury has in its Museum, in addition to the Hob-nob or Hobby Horse (p.46) a Giant, who today is normally only brought out for royal occasions, such as coronations and jubilees. I have seen him in procession in the streets of Salisbury three or four times in my life. He is about twelve feet high, with a swarthy complexion, a black, bushy beard and huge staring eyes. He is carried by a bearer hidden beneath his full, mediaeval robes. Records dating from the Middle Ages refer to him as St Christopher. Jean Morrison, after pointing out that the giant may belong to an earlier tradition goes on to add:

> At some time in the Middle Ages he was appropriated by the Tailors' Guild, whose patronal festival fell on 24 June, Midsummer Day. We do not know exactly how old he is, but he went in the procession led by the Mayor and Corporation to meet Henry VII and his Queen in 1496, and he was old then. He was an important figure in all celebrations, particularly St John's (Midsummer) Night, St Osmund's Night (16 July) and St Peter's Night (1 August), all summer festivals, when he was accompanied by Hob-nob, his esquires bearing mace, sword and lantern, the Morris dancers, three black boys and a devil. All were elaborately dressed in clothes provided by the Tailors' Guild.

In the nineteenth century the Giant and Hob-nob made frequent appearances in Salisbury, and Jean Morrison suggests that they were not always especially stately or decorous:

> 'while the bearers of the Giant refreshed themselves (in a pub) the Morris dancers became the centre of attraction, dancing to traditional tunes, three dressed as men in streamers and bells, and three as women, and one as a fool. Then, when the collecting box had gone round, and thirst was satisfied, the procession continued on its way, perhaps a little less steadily. And all the way the two flautists played old tunes, which were half-drowned by the heavy thud of the drum representing the sound of the Giant's footsteps, and Hob-nob rushed about, jaws snapping, chasing the girls and making them squeal with pretended fright, his bearer's blackened face, half hidden under helmet and veil, adding to the terrifying appearance of the black horse.'

I well remember marching, as a schoolboy, in procession behind the Giant and hearing that sombre thudding of the drum.

The devil is a familiar figure in Wiltshire folklore. He

appeared in the form of a hare when two men were hanged on Warminster Down in 1813, and later in the same century he attended the Palm Sunday gathering on Cowdown, Longbridge Deverill, this time as a dog. 'Sum'at wer there, anyhow,' and they all ran away. 'After that there were no more gatherings'. A story noted down in 1889 described how a

Deverill man was courting in Hindon, and he walked home down Lord's Hill, and he seed sum'at, and he said, 'If thou be the devil, appear bodily;' and he seed sum'at as had eyes as big as a tea-saucer; he didn't know how he got home, and the sweat poured down him like rain, and every single hair of his head did stand on end, and he never seed the going on't.

Lord's Hill is supposed to be the spot where a Jew was murdered. Local people refused him a burial in the churchyard, so he was buried outside, to the north, at a point which became known as 'the Jew's Wall'.

The Devil is said to have been responsible for at least three prominent Wiltshire hills. One legend concerns Cley Hill, near Warminster. The Devil was angry with the people of Devizes, so he went to Somerset and fetched a big 'hump' to throw at the town. On his way back he stopped an old man near Warminster to enquire his way. The answer was: 'That's just what I want to know myself. I started for Devizes when my beard was black, and now its grey and I haven't got there yet.'

This so discouraged the Devil that he flung his sack of earth away and there it still is, in the form of Cley Hill.

A similar tale is told of Silbury (p.23). Here it was Marlborough which had angered the Devil and was going to be buried, but magic performed by priests at Avebury forced him to dump his sack of soil, which formed Silbury Hill.

Another version of the legend has Avebury itself in danger, though the cause of the Devil's irritation was Stonehenge. Robert Heanley, placing on record a story said to have been current in a Melksham family for at least three centuries, published it in *Folk-Lore* (1913) in the original words:

When Stonehenge was builded, a goodish bit after Avebury, the devil were in a rare taking. 'There's getting a vast deal too much religion in those here parts,' he says, 'summat must be done.' So he picks up his shovel, and cuts a slice out of Salisbury Plain, and sets off for to smother up Avebury. But the priests saw him coming and set to work with their charms and incusstations, and they fixed him while he wer yet a nice way off, till at last he flings down his shovelful just where he stood. And *that's* Silbuty.

Another tradition, collected from a different source, has it that a horseman in golden armour lies buried beneath the hill, complete with his mount.

Sidbury Hill near Everley, entirely distinct from the above, was dropped by the Devil on his way to Bristol. There is said to be a well in Everley with an opening in its side, and from this a tunnel leads into the heart of Sidbury Hill. With the added detail that a golden chair stands there, waiting to be discovered, the whole story sounds rather as if it had been confused with Silbury. Thirty or so barrows in the vicinity are explained by Everley people as burial places of those 'killed in the battle of Sidbury Hill.'

In addition to its connections with the Devil, Wiltshire claims to possess a feather from the wing of the Archangel Gabriel. In the parish church at Pewsey a glazed recess in one of the pillars of the nave contains what appear to be goose feathers. An inscription reads:

This recess was discovered at the Restoration of the Church in 1800. It then enclosed some feathers which are now replaced. Its object is uncertain, but probably it was a reliquary supposed to contain feathers dropt by the Archangel Gabriel in the Temple, as many churches on the Continent, dedicated to St John the Baptist, have such reliquaries.

William of Malmesbury records as authentic the story of a monk, Elmer, who tried to emulate the Archangel:

He was a man of good learning for those times, of mature age, and in his early youth had hazarded an attempt of singular temerity. He had by some contrivance fastened wings to his hands and feet, in order that, looking upon the fable as true, he might fly like Daedalus, and collecting the air on the summit of a tower, had flown for more than the distance of a furlong; but, agitated by the violence of the wind and the current of air, he fell and broke both his legs, and was lame ever after. He used to relate as the cause of his failure, his forgetting to provide himself with a tail.

The tower in question belonged to Malmesbury Abbey and is supposed to have taken place in Saxon times, for the story is recorded as incidental to a prophecy uttered by Elmer on seeing Halley's Comet, just before the Norman Conquest.

A similar story to that of Lyddie Shears is told of a witch of Tidcombe. A farm foreman shot at and wounded a hare, and on the same day an old woman suspected of being a witch became ill and died.

9　Funerals and Ghosts

DEATH WAS A MORE frequent occurrence in villages of a century ago than it is today. Village mothers were asked how many children they had reared, rather than how many they had had. An old man who must have been born about 1850, at Pitton, told me that he remembered three of his small sisters lying dead at the same time in his house. They had succumbed to an epidemic of 'fever' – possibly scarlet fever.

When death was imminent it was said that dogs howled, owls hooted and cats left the house. It was a bad omen for a robin to enter a building where a person lay sick, and the same applied to rats and mice. A guttering candle which sends down a cascade of melted wax was supposed to be preparing a winding sheet.

An observer in one remote Wiltshire village noted that, during the 19th century, mistrust of corpses was strong, and people were very unwilling to enter churchyards at night. Apparently these anxieties were diminishing by the end of the century, as was fear of ghosts, most of whom were thought to have been laid by the local clergyman.

On the other hand, a local squire had his wife's corpse placed in the coach house after death, and there was a general dislike of keeping a body in the dwelling. A dying man might ask for his knife to be placed on the hob, the result hoped for being an easy death.

Until the second world war the passing bell was always tolled when a parishioner died in my native village, Pitton. Men working in the fields would hear it and discuss the identity of the deceased. The custom of 'watching with the dead', on the night after the death, was discontinued somewhat earlier. The coffin was left open until the day of the funeral, so that neighbours and relatives could come to 'view' the corpse. It was thought that by examining the face of a dead person, it was possible to judge what his situation in the future life might be. All blinds were drawn in the houses along the road over which the corpse was taken to the graveyard. The funeral procession travelled slowly, and no-one would dream of overtaking it. Anyone who did so was said to be hurrying to his own grave. Men whom it passed in the street stood still and raised their hats.

When it came to the actual burial, caution had to be observed in not placing hostile relatives in nearby graves, for fear that the contention might carry on into after life. A women who suffered a leg amputation had the limb interred in a special little coffin, and gave instructions that she herself was to be buried as close to it as possible. Her friends explained that 'she would have to be sharp in claiming her leg on the Day of Judgement lest someone else, maimed in the same way, should seize it before her.'

Until the first world war the custom of wearing black armbands was widespread, and black-edged mourning cards were in common use. Black-edged paper was also used by the bereaved family for letter writing for some time after the death.

Parish registers reveal occasional references to corpses buried in wool, in accordance with the seventeenth-century Act of Parliament designed to assist the wool trade. A shepherd would be buried with a tuft of wool on his shroud, so that when he presented himself at the gates of heaven St Peter would recognise him as a shepherd and would excuse him for non-attendance at church on Sundays. Miss Law heard of this custom being observed at the end of the last century, in the case of a shearer.

Excavations in the 1950s of a series of mounds and ditches on the downs above Pitton revealed the burial ground of the inhabitants of a Roman-British village. The corpses, some inhumations and some cremations, were buried around the inner rim of a crescent-shaped earthwork, around a central pit of unkown significance. Several of the intact skeletons had coins of the fourth century AD, so positioned that they had evidently been placed in the mouths of the deceased. The excavators said that these would be to pay the toll to the ferryman who would take their souls across the dark river, an idea which certainly existed at various places in the past. The exact circumstances of these burials are, of course, unknown.

Sometimes there seems to have been a certain disapproval of barrow excavations, linked, just possibly, with anxiety. Professor Charles Thomas felt this when digging near Everley in 1953, and he was told that William Cunnington and his colleagues, who had done similar work in 1805, had been put in prison as a result. Of course this was untrue, though the story must reflect popular disapproval at disturbing the dead. Professor Thomas was given the information by an old shepherd, aged 77, who worked on Snail Down near the barrows. He in turn had it as a boy from an old man, who died at 93, and who could actually remember seeing William Cunnington's excavations. Since Professor Thomas was there in 1953, 148 years after Cunnington's work, and since 93 plus 77 totals 170, the two informants probably averaged about 11 years old when they, respectively, perceived or heard of the 1805 dig. It is as Professor Thomas says, an interesting example of an account given at only second hand after an interval of almost 150 years; also of how short a chain of informants is needed to underwrite error, in the best possible faith.

The chalk downs are associated with memories of early battles. One is said to have been fought at Marden, between the Saxons and Danes. According to local legend black-haired men were conquered by red-haired men, presumed to be the Danes. Within living memory red-haired children in certain villages in west Wiltshire have been called 'Daners'. On the downs near Bowerchalke is a hollow known as Patty's Bottom.

Here Romans and Britons are said to have fought, till the valley ran with blood. Miss Olivier, who collected the information from local people, writes: 'On certain moonlight nights tramping is distinctly heard, and horses without heads can be seen rushing madly about.' A little man in a red hat has been reported from time to time in All Cannings, but this is more likely to be a description of a fairy, since they traditionally wore this colour.

Kathleen Wiltshire, author of *Ghosts and Legends of the Wiltshire Countryside,* relates that 'an old shepherd who used to keep his flocks on Cherhill Down told me he had seen "a lot of men a-marchin'," adding, "they did wear skirts!" "*Were* they men?" I asked. "Oh yes, they did have beards, some on 'em, and they wore girt helmets – wi' 'air across the top . . . and had a girt bird on a pole a 'front on 'em!" ' This sounds like an account of a Roman legion marching along the road that runs over the down, but it is possible that the old man had at some time seen a picture of Roman soldiers in action. A centurion is also said to walk along the Ridgeway above Market Lavington.

Other apparitions, including various monks and nuns, date from the Middle Ages. For example, certain churches are haunted by nuns – Highworth, Stratton St Margaret and others. A 'grey' ghost seen at Beckington Abbey is thought to be a former abbess, and a nun walks in the Priory of St Mary at Kington St Michael. A monk is said to mount the staircase known as the Monk's Stair at Fyfield Manor, near Pewsey. Others use the underground passages thought to connect St Mary's Church at Cricklade with the old Priory. More ghostly monks haunt local taverns – the Royal Oak at Corsley and an inn at Highworth – and the spectre of a monk at Edington walks in a garden on the site of the old monastery.

All Cannings is said to have a 'grey lady', identified as Elizabeth Bynge, wife of the Rev. Robert Bynge who built the Rectory (where she has been seen on several occasions) in 1645. Elizabeth was born in All Cannings, married there and had three small sons when the Civil War broke out. Because of her husband's known Royalist sympathies the family were turned out of their home under the Commonwealth.

A cottage in the same village is haunted by Ruth King. She was apparently rather an eccentric old lady, reputed to have some money hidden in her cottage. But nothing could be found when she died. She is said to have come back on several occasions, to reveal her treasure or to see that it was still safe. Once, when repairs were being done, the carpenter found a cardboard box inside a cavity. There was great excitement, but the box contained nothing except the old lady's stays, an empty purse, and a few knick-knacks.

Kathleen Wiltshire describes a fairly recent incident which took place in 1946 or 1947. An old man, Joshua Cowdry, went to Devizes Hospital and one afternoon his neighbours were surprised to see him walk up his garden path and go into his cottage. Later they learned that he had died in the hospital just at that time. She has a not dissimilar story of a well-known parishioner of Potterne who used to pay supposedly secret visits to a widow in the village – though in fact everyone knew about it. He was seen walking up her path as usual a fortnight after his death.

Many years ago, at Wilcot, in the same district, Dame Anne Wroughton, was turned out into the snow because her husband suspected her, falsely, of being unfaithful. She died of exposure, and since then her ghost has been seen from time to time by villagers, who call her 'The White Lady of Wilcot'. Wilcot Manor itself is haunted by the ghost of a monk said to be one of the last to live there at the time of the Dissolution, in the sixteenth century. He hanged himself rather than leave his old home.

Country mansions are often thought to be haunted and Longleat has several ghosts. One is the Green Lady, supposed to be Lady Louisa Carteret, second wife of the second Lord Weymouth. Her husband, having learned, so it is said, that she had a lover, fought a duel with a man in the passage now known as the Green Lady's Walk. The man was killed and his body was buried within the house. It may have been his remains which were discovered during alterations to the mansion in the present century, but it is the lady's ghost, not his, which is said to walk. Sir John Thynne, who built the house, has been seen at Longleat; so has the saintly Bishop Ken, who hid there from religious persecution in the seventeenth century.

During the late 1940s two children were left at Corsham Priory with the housekeeper while their parents were abroad. When the grown-ups returned, one of the children could recite the Ave Maria, which he claimed to have learned from 'a man in white'; about 200 years before this event the Priory had been occupied by an order of white friars.

Littlecote has a legend that when the heir is about to die Wild Will Darrell, mentioned earlier, drives up to the door in his coach. In about 1861 little Francis Popham, who was six months old, was lying dangerously ill when his nurse heard a coach and horses approaching the house. Thinking that it was the boy's parents, she looked out of the window and saw nothing. That night the child died. His parents did not arrive till the following day.

One night during the second world war an evacuee at Whetham House, near Calne, was woken up by a man beside his bed. He jumped up and tried to seize him only to find there was nothing there. The man, so he said, was dressed in a tall hat and cloak. He was not the first to have seen this ghost, believed to be a Russian killed years ago in a duel.

The wife of Sir Ferdinando Blunt, lord of the manor at Lydiard Millicent, had a lover before her marriage who was curate of the parish. He was murdered in her presence, the date being October 30th, and on the anniversary she is sometimes seen sitting under a tree in the garden of the Manor House.

Some time during the second or third decades of this century a Miss Coles, niece of the rector of Manningford Bruce, woke up one night and saw several gentlemen in Stuart clothes, one resembling Charles I, playing cards by the fireplace in her bedroom in the Rectory. She dozed off again, woke a little later and found them still playing their game. The episode suggests that Miss Coles was a lady of serene disposition, unless, of course, she was dreaming. Boscombe also has a ghost in its Rectory, said to be a man who hanged himself in the attic.

Various Wiltshire churches have their own ghost stories. Once, while officiating at Communion in the Saxon church of St. Lawrence at Bradford-on-Avon, the Vicar noticed a large group of people dressed in mediaeval clothes and standing near the altar rail. At Wilcot a women saw the apparition of her father, an archdeacon who had recently died, standing behind the officiating clergyman during the Communion Service.

Allington, near Salisbury, is haunted by a curate who died 150 years or so ago. The official story of his death is that, after an evening spent with friends, he tried to mount his horse but fell off and broke his neck. Apparently this was not strictly accurate: on her deathbed, many years later, a woman who had been present said she wished to tell what had really happened, but before she could explain she grew suddenly much worse and died in agony.

Calne parish church has eight bells. Sometimes, when only seven ringers have arrived, disembodied footsteps are heard coming up the tower. A ghost is arriving to complete the team.

There are various haunted inns. Harry Jones, landlord of the King's Arms at Malmesbury for forty years until 1920, has been heard breathing heavily in the bedroom where he died; sometimes he walks about, turning off beer taps and switching on lights. The Old Bell inn, also at Malmesbury and on the edge of the old Abbey precincts, is haunted by a 'grey lady'. She has been seen both inside and outside, and if she passes through the hedge the bushes always die just at that spot.

The Haunch of Venison, one of Salisbury's oldest inns, dates from about 1320. It has a 'white lady', who walks in the graveyard behind the back windows. Nell Gwynne once slept at the Phoenix at Pewsey, and a woman in Restoration costume has since been reported there. It is said to be her, but who can be sure, since the apparition has no head?

At Swindon there have been some curious occurrences reported from the Clifton Hotel. Wine glasses move across the bar without breaking. A dog present on one of these occasions became thoroughly scared. The hotel is believed to stand on the site of an ancient priory.

Stanton St Bernard has its own dramatic story of a farmer's wife, buried a century or so ago in the family vault. The sexton had noticed the valuable rings that she was wearing and decided to steal them. After the funeral, when it was dark, he went down into the vault, prised open the coffin and took them. One ring stuck, so he cut off the whole finger with his knife. To his horror the body sat up! He ran away, leaving his lantern, so the woman picked it up and walked back home, the wound dripping blood as she went. Each year on the anniversary of the funeral she is said to walk along the road from the church to the farm and appear in the dining-room, where her husband had been sitting when she returned. Her finger still drips blood. Stories of this kind are not unusual and are linked with premature burial. This did occur in the days when it was still difficult to establish whether someone was really dead or just in a coma.

Reginald de Cobham, of Langley Burrell, burnt as a heretic in the fifteenth century, walks naked and, curiously, since he was not decapitated, with his head under his arm. The drummer-boy of Salisbury Plain haunts, or used to haunt, a fork road at West Lavington. He was murdered there, for his pay, by a colour sergeant. Years later the sergeant returned to the spot and hearing the boy's drum, confessed to his crime. This may be a good example of a guilty conscience at work.

Lonely Chute Causeway, which follows the line of a Roman road, not far from the Hampshire village of Vernham Dean, is haunted by the ghost of a rector of Chute. During an outbreak of plague in the reign of Charles II this rector persuaded those of his parishioners who had contracted the illness to isolate themselves in a camp he had established on the hill by the Causeway. He promised to supply them with food and other necessities but then abandoned them. Most of them died from starvation or disease. After he himself caught the plague and died, his ghost was often seen trudging up the hill towards the camp.

Hill Deverill has a ghost who, according to local tradition, is Sir Henry Coker, 'Old Coker', who died in 1736 and still gallops around the parish with his hounds. He lived at Manor Farm, situated beside a marsh made by the river Deverill, in a lonely and dreary spot. Parts of the building were probably Tudor, and local tradition (1889) regarded it as a place where 'traitors were shut up'. Coker himself had the reputation of a smuggler and robber, 'and many went into the house that never came out'. There were bloodstains on the floor in one bedroom. The house was 'like a den of thieves', and he 'used to go about at night with men and rob. He kept a cannon at the round window.'

These were the recollections of local people about a century-and-a-half after Sir Henry's death, implying that he was exactly the type of personality to whom ghost stories attach. And indeed, he could still sometimes be seen, sitting 'on the dreshol (threshold) of the barn, so that they had to go in another way', or riding through the grounds near the house, 'horses galloping and chains rattling', with his horn sounding. On other occasions he had been heard driving his hounds round 'Gun's Church', a barrow in the south-east of the parish, and here his name became associated with the 'Spectral Hunt', a widespread motif in European folklore. It is also known as 'The Wild Hunt'.

Sir Henry was remembered in neighbouring parishes too. In Brixton Deverill, to the south, he continued to haunt a house until it was altered: 'Old Coker did come again'. Possibly a belief at Longbridge Deverill, that kegs of brandy would roll at night-time from a certain thicket in Church Lane, derived from his smuggling associations. At any rate, local people avoided the lane after dark, where another anxiety was a rain of woolpacks from the same thicket.

James Waylen's *A History of Marlborough* (1854) tells the story of Edward Avon and Thomas Goddard, as taken from a deposition made before the Mayor, Town Clerk and Rector of Marlbourgh in 1674 by Thomas Goddard. It describes how the spirit of Edward Avon appeared to Thomas Goddard, his son-in-law, on several occasions and instructed him to rectify certain wrongs perpetrated by Avon during his lifetime. The deposition was made on November 23rd, 1674, and concerned several occurrences between November 9th and that date. Avon had died in the preceding May.

On the first occasion, which was in broad daylight, at nine o'clock in the morning, Avon tried to get Goddard to accept some money, which he claimed to have withheld from his daughter Sarah. After one or two further visitations, Avon appeared to Goddard again in the open fields and gave him specific detailed instructions on certain matters. Goddard was requested to tell William Avon, Edward's son, to pay money owing to his sister Sarah, to a man to whom he had owed money and to 'little Sarah Taylor', who may have been his unacknowledged illegitimate child. Furthermore, William Avon was to take his father's sword to a place in the woods, where Edward would meet him.

All this was done, and when Thomas and William Avon went to the woods the next morning Edward appeared, accompanied by something 'like a mastiff dog of brown colour'. The ghost of Edward Avon then took them farther into the woods and required them to put down the sword in a place where, he said, 'lies buried the body of him which I murdered in the year 1635, which is now rotten and turned to dust . . . I took money from the man, and he contended with me, and so I murdered him.' Apart from the deposition made to the town dignitaries, nothing is recorded of any sequel to this story. It is perhaps interesting to mention that Avon said he had, in the other world, 'received mercy contrary to my deserts'.

Another story of ghostly intervention in human affairs relates how in 1592 the second wife of Sir Walter Long, M.P., of Draycot, and her brother conspired to persuade Sir Walter to disinherit the rightful heir, his son by his first wife, in favour of the second wife's son. Sir Walter's lawyer was drawing up the will when a lady's white hand appeared and prevented him. This was presumably the hand of the first wife. In the end a compromise was agreed.

S. Jackson Coleman, author of *Folk Lore of Wiltshire*, tells the story of 'Wild Cunliffe', said to haunt the ruins of Wycoller Hall, near Calne. He was a wild young man who killed his beautiful wife because he thought she was the cause of his bad luck at gambling. On the anniversary of the murder people say he returns to the scene of his crime. Riding a phantom horse he gallops up to the Hall, dismounts and goes upstairs with his sword drawn. Terrible screams are heard, the rider reappears, mounts his horse and gallops away.

Sometimes ghost stories are linked with the finding of human remains. Two children staying at a house in Lacock were frightened by an 'ugly little man' who walked through their room. Many years later a skeleton was found under the bedroom wall. A house in Corsham was haunted by an old man who used to appear from a wall. When the building was demolished, the skeleton of a man was found in a cavity. The skeletons of five children were discovered when the wing of the old manor house at Sutton Veny was pulled down. A woman who slept there some time ago thought she felt a child's head resting on her shoulder in bed for two consecutive nights.

Another skeleton found bricked in a wall was of a woman in a cottage at Upavon; it was discovered when the building was pulled down. Her ghost appeared each year on Lady Day, the day on which residents would probably have moved out. Where the road from Lavington starts to climb to the downs a headless woman, dressed in white, with a red cloak, is sometimes seen. During alterations to the cemetery at the end of last century the skeleton of a woman, with the head missing, was found.

Pinkney Park, near Sherston, has a skull said to be that of a member of the Pinkney family from which the estate takes its name. It is kept in a niche above the stairs and is thought, because of its small size, to be female. Local tradition says that many attempts have been made to destroy this skull, by burning, smashing with a hammer and sundry other methods, but it defies them all. The legend adds that when the last Pinkney dies and the estate passes into other hands, the skull will, of its own accord, crumble into dust. Unfortunately for the legend, the estate has not been owned by the Pinkney family for centuries. Why anyone should take so much trouble to try to destroy a skull is not recorded.

About a hundred years ago a ghost caused havoc at Wyke House, Trowbridge, and attracted so much publicity that twelve Anglican clergymen were summoned to exorcise it. The ghost was invited to choose its place of exile, so it asked for a certain large chest to be brought, stepped inside and was sealed in.

John Powell questioned local people in Heytesbury Parish between 1889 and 1894 about the laying of a ghost there in 1854. This was a member of one of the leading local families, evidently not very long dead at the time. 'Parson Smith' performed the laying, though all the local clergy had been summoned 'to conjure it'. But all the others were 'mastered', and they 'gied out'. In fact, had it not been for Parson Smith, 'they would have been torn to pieces'. Dismemberment by ghosts was evidently widely expected, for on one occasion a shepherd at Roundway, on being accompanied for some distance by a headless apparition, remained silent for fear that 'if I hadn't spoken proper to him he'd a tore 'un to pieces'.

Apparently the Heytesbury ghost's wife had asked for the exorcism, though, according to one informant, she had habitually talked with her dead husband once a year, wearing a sheepskin inside out. This was evidently a protection against ghosts, and was more often referred to simply as a 'lambs skin'. 'A spirit will tear you in pieces if you do not answer its questions, but it will not hurt a lamb's skin.'

Another opinion, that a spirit cannot address you until you have spoken to it, implies that any such untoward results could only follow if the living person had first taken the initiative. The words to use – and, no doubt, those used by Parson Smith – are: 'In the name of the Lord, why troublest thou here?' After conversation, the spirit asked, 'What is the simplest thing in the world?' The Parson said, 'A lamb'. Then the ghost was laid. The Parson wanted to lay the ghost in the Red Sea, but the ghost begged not to be put there. Powell adds: 'On that night there was a fearful storm; my informant's house was "unheled" (thatch blown off). When there was a great tempest, people used to say, "They're conjuring".'

Stories of headless horsemen and phantom coaches were once very popular. Today many ghost legends have collected around their successor, the motor car, a popular symbol of modern culture. A Great Bedwyn resident is convinced that she once gave a ghost a lift in her car. One wet night when she was driving along the road to Newbury she passed a figure in white, and immediately afterwards became very cold and had a feeling that someone was sitting behind her, in the back seat. The chill suddenly disappeared again when she reached Newbury.

Another encounter between a car and a ghost occurred near Atworth one winter evening, when a Bath taxi driver jammed on his brakes, to avoid a horseman crossing the road. But the horseman vanished. One morning at six o'clock a car driver nearly ran into a pedestrian near Hullavington. He tried to stop the car, but seemed to be prevented from doing so. He had a clear view of the man, who then vanished. This occurred near a spot where, according to local tradition, a coach once overturned in a pond – now filled in – drowning the passengers.

A cyclist making his way across the downs from Durnford to Amesbury one moonlit night in winter heard a horseman galloping towards him. It crossed the road just in front of him, but he saw nothing. Two phantom cars have been recorded. One is a blue Morris Minor which appears near Shockerwick Bridge, on the Bath road. Traffic drives through it. Another is an American, seen speeding up a hill near Pickwick, with no driver. In the 1920s a Seend man saw a phantom bus near the village. It disappeared without trace.

In the days of ponies and traps two Methodist local preachers were returning from a service one Sunday evening when, near Allington (Devizes), they met a girl in white, walking through heavy rain. They thought of offering her a lift, but when they drew level with her, she disappeared.

Several ghostly funeral processions have been seen in Wiltshire. One was near Potterne, in the early years of this century, and a procession of mourners followed the coffin. An old man told the person who witnessed the sight that he himself had often seen it on the same spot. At Ramsbury a coffin is carried along a road by two headless men. At Stockley, near Calne, a man stood at the roadside, cap in hand, to wait for an approaching funeral procession to pass, but just before it reached him it vanished. Near Bratton a funeral carriage drawn by horses has occasionally been seen.

Some ghosts appear on the open downs, well away from human dwellings and roads, and the witnesses are often shepherds. In the nineteenth century two shepherds on Tan Hill, in All Cannings parish, saw what appears to have been a royal funeral procession. Kathleen Wiltshire describes what happened:

> It was a dark night, and suddenly they heard sounds as of men and horses coming towards them along the Wansdyke. This would have been most unusual, even in daylight. Then the moon shone out from behind a cloud, and they could see a party of men, carrying torches, and walking behind a waggon drawn by black horses. On the waggon was strapped a coffin, on top of which lay a crown, or circle of gold . . . When the cortege drew level with them it vanished . . .

On Knook Down many years ago a shepherd reported seeing lights 'bobbing up and down'. In consequence, 'the Government people sent soldiers', who apparently unearthed 'guns and swords and dead bodies, and, where the lights were, a large box of valuables and money'.

Another story concerns labourers who, according to Edith Olivier,

> were working in Old Down Barn, on Durnford Down, near Oozens Hill, where they were winnowing corn, the barn doors being trigged open very securely to prevent them coming to. The sheep were grazing on the downs in front of the barn quite peacefully, when suddenly there seemed to spring up a sudden squall on an otherwise calm and sunny day. The workmen thought it was the bailiff coming (goodness knows why!) but could see nothing; the sheep suddenly parted in the middle and ran hither and thither in

a terrified condition. A galloping horse appeared to go
through the sheep, and the men distinctly heard the
'scrooping' noise made by the leather saddle. The barn
doors slammed together, as though by some unseen hand
. . . and the galloping of the horse grew fainter and finally
ceased.

Many ghost stories are concerned with animals, especially
dogs, cats and horses. Sometimes the animals see the
apparition; sometimes they appear in this form. Ghostly black
dogs are particularly numerous. Many of their haunts are by
old tracks and roadways or by derelict buildings. Kathleen
Wiltshire, who has made a collection of black dog stories, lists
45 for Wiltshire.

Two interesting legends are told about the black dogs of
Chapmanslade. One was trained by a highwayman to jump
from the bank of a sunken lane and attack passing coachmen,
who were then robbed by its master. Eventually the dog was
shot by a guard hired specially, but its ghost returned to haunt
the spot. The other tale is of two men courting the same girl at
Black Dog Farm. They had a fight, and one was killed. The
black dog belonging to the dead man then attacked the winner
and killed him, and the girl, hearing of the tragedy, committed
suicide. One must assume that the dog was also killed, for its
ghost still haunts the place.

The black dogs at Foxham and Wootton Bassett appear as
a warning of death, illness or some other calamity; and during
the upheaval of the second world war a large black dog was
seen at midnight on a bridge near Pewsey, led on a sparkling
chain by a lady in black.

A phantom Alsatian – and therefore, one supposes, not
black – caused serious trouble at a Swindon council house
within the last decade. A spiritualist, Mrs Anne Reilly, had
earlier been the tenant but vacated the premises, which were
in Penhill Drive, before the problems occurred. While she was
living there her pets, the dog and her cat, both died, though
she later saw them walking about the house. The next
occupants, a family of four, also suffered from animal
apparitions and complained of things moving about for no
obvious reason. Once, one of the children was pinned to a wall
by an unseen force. Mrs Reilly thought that the 'happenings'
could have been caused by her two dead pets. At any rate the

family left in terror, and Swindon Council refused to reallocate the house until it had been exorcised by a clergyman. All this was reported by the *Daily Express* on 6 April 1966.

Wiltshire has its share of ghostly pigs. At Calcutt, near Cricklade, on Christmas Eve little piglets with red ears, a fairy colour, run across the road. Bishops Cannings has an enormous phantom sow which crosses Pig Lane. Some say she pushes a barrel in front of her. One night at Manningford Abbotts a woman living in the Rectory looked out of her bedroom window and saw a woman driving a pig across the lawn. As she watched, both vanished.

Birds are often linked with death and there is a strange story told about an ornithologist Rev. W. Fowler, who retired to a Wiltshire rectory to write a book on the subject. As he lay dying,

all the owls in the neighbourhood seemed to have gathered around his house, perching on the roof, gateposts, pinnacles or any convenient place. They remained there till he was dead, when they all disappeared. On the day of the funeral, however, when the coffin was being carried under the lych-gate to the church, a large white barn owl swooped down almost touching the coffin before disappearing into the large yew tree in the churchyard.

Wiltshire has had several poltergeists. Perhaps the most celebrated is the phantom bell of Wilcot, which performed long enough to become nationally famous in the reign of James I. People made pilgrimages to hear it, and it is said that the king himself sent a delegate to make a report. The culprit was a Devizes wizard named Cantle. One night in 1624 a drunken man arrived at the vicarage door and demanded to be allowed to ring the church bells. Naturally the vicar refused, and the drunkard went away, muttering threats of revenge. He was still harbouring his grievance some time later when he met Cantle who said: 'Does the vicar love ringing? He shall have enough of it.' From that time the bell never stopped ringing in the vicar's bedroom. Outside the house it could not be heard, and the ringing could be lost by putting one's head out of the window. Cantle, arrested and lodged in Salisbury

Gaol, said that the ringing would continue till his death, and it did.

At Newton Tony many years ago a poltergeist took possession of a cottage bread oven. When they were in bed at night the residents heard a clatter as if the oven itself had fallen out and was rolling about the floor. China used to be shaken off the dresser by the commotion. At last the housewife called in the village bricklayer to put things right. Edith Olivier says:

> This he did, but while examining the inside of the oven he found an old wooden bowl, round, such as were then used as tills in old inns. This he took home as a curio, declaring it was empty. He had, however, a deaf and dumb daughter, and she told by signs to a friend that it had lots and lots of money in it. Anyway, the bricklayer was never short of cash afterwards, and the cottage ceased from having oven and china rolling about.

Another group of stories about the supernatural concerns people who have seen things, especially buildings, that belong to an earlier period. Kathleen Wiltshire quotes a letter written by a Mr. T. Siree, of Chelmsford:

> My parents had rented a cottage in Savernake for the summer. We had just come back from India, where we went during the first year of my life. I was then eight years of age. The cottage had been rented through an advertisement, and there was no connection between us and the locality. When we drove up I asked my parents why we were arriving at the back door, only to be told the back door was on the other side, by the kitchen. I was puzzled by the staircase, which I maintained was the servants', not 'our' stairs. It was pointed out that there was only one staircase in the cottage; I persisted that there was another staricase, and lots more rooms, where then only stretched a blank wall, cutting off a shrubbery, which grew right up to the house.

My mother found out that the cottage was indeed all that was left of a large coaching inn that had been burnt down some fifty years before. Only the servants' quarters had been saved, and no attempt had been made to rebuild the main part, as the need for so large a place had passed . . .

To this day I can draw the plan of the original house, which I know in detail, and which subsequently proved to be wholly accurate."

A remarkable story is told by Edna Hedges of an event that occurred in the 1930s, when she was in her early teens. One Sunday afternoon she cycled from Hannington to Wanborough to visit a friend, passing along a road that was a section of the ancient Ermine Street. Halfway along, she was caught in a torrential storm and so, seeing a thatched cottage a little way up a lane, she went there and asked for shelter.

A tall old man, with long grey hair and beard and a pipe in his mouth, beckoned her inside. She sat by a fire which burned in an old-fashioned grate, and the old man stood smiling at her but did not speak. When the storm was over she went on her way. At Wanborough her friends were surprised to see her arrive bone-dry. When she told how she had taken refuge in the cottage they were puzzled. They told her that there was no cottage on that road – only a derelict one which had been empty for fifty years.

A week or two later Mrs Hedges passed that way again and saw her cottage. 'More than half the thatch had caved in, leaving rafters exposed to the sky; the door hung askew on the hinges, the broken panes were green and murky. What had once been a garden was more of a jungle; the smell of decay was everywhere . . . '

A somewhat similar tale is told, more recently, of a girl who went for a walk on Tan Hill, near the Wansdyke. On her return she described a house she had seen, with every sign of occupation, including a horse looking over a stable door and chicken scratching in the yard. But no-one had ever heard of a house there, and when she went to look for it again she could not find it. Years later, someone found an old book with an illustration of Tan Hill, showing a house just where the girl had seen it.

Several stories describe mysterious lights. At Market Lavington in 1938 a gleam from a Gothic window was seen in a wall where there is no window, only a fireplace; and a glow as in a stained glass window at Upavon proved on investigation to have appeared in a place where there was not only no window but no building. It was later discovered that this had been the site of an old Benedictine monastery.

This is a selection of Wiltshire ghost stories, and I have tried to include all the best known. In her book *Ghosts and Legends of the Wiltshire Countryside* Kathleen Wiltshire lists 275 and even that is not complete. For instance, I know three from my native village, Pitton, which she does not mention. One is of an invisible ghost which has made its presence felt, by the rustling of curtains, chilly draughts and movements of furniture, at intervals of more than a century. These occurrences have been reported recently from a house which is fairly modern but is on the site of one much older. A sense of menace pervades, at night, a deep cutting in the chalk, overhung by yew-trees, on the road from Pitton to Farley. When this road was widened in about the middle of the nineteenth century the workmen found a grave, in which lay the skeleton of a man with a knife by his side. It was know locally as 'The Gypsy's Grave', though on what grounds I do not know. Then there were the two men, still alive when I was a boy, who said they had been walking through Clarendon Woods one snowy night when they saw a woman walking ahead of them. Not recognising her, they hurried to catch her up, to satisfy their curiosity. As they drew nearer she disappeared, and, looking down at the snow, they saw she had left no footprints.

These are just a few of the stories that I happen to know because I lived in Pitton for fifty years. I suspect that almost every village in the county could match my modest score.

One delightful story in conclusion is a pleasant contrast to some of the more sinister and gruesome spectres recorded above. Philipps' House at Dinton is a fine country mansion now used for educational courses by several organisations. Once the home of the Wyndham family, today it belongs to the National Trust. A feature of the building is the impressive staircase with balustrade, descending to a spacious hall. Not long ago a woman attending a course came out of her bedroom at about midnight and saw the elegant figure of a lady in flimsy clothes descending the staircase. The next day, she naturally told her story, and her companions watched for the ghost on subsequent nights, without success.

At the social evening on the final night of the course, another member of the group confessed:

I hope you will forgive me but that magnificent stairway fascinated me. I thought of Regency ladies floating down the steps on their way to a ball, with the horse and carriages waiting outside. What a wonderful feeling it must have been, I thought! So I just had to try it for myself. That night I put on my prettiest night-dress and a floral dressing-gown, and when I thought everyone was asleep I walked down the stairs to my imaginary carriage. I didn't know that anyone had seen me.

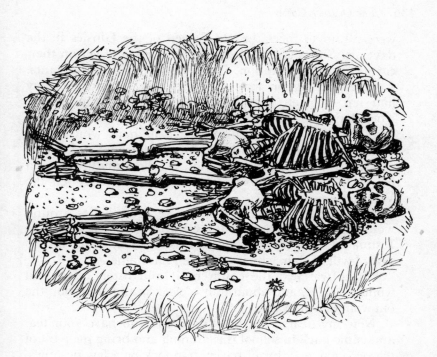

10   The Odstock Curse

ONE OF THE MOST DRAMATIC stories of old Wiltshire concerns the Odstock Curse. I came across it in the 1930s, when I was given a copy of the chronicle written by an eye-witness of most of the events, the village blacksmith of Odstock, Hiram Witt. The story seems to begin about the year 1798, and Hiram Witt wrote his account in the year 1870. Certain sequels to it were added in 1930 by his son-in-law – at least I believe that was their relationship.

The story is now widely known, particularly since I wrote a radio play around it, which was broadcast in the early 1950s. Hiram Witt's original version has, however, a dramatic quality which would be difficult to surpass and is quite remarkable from the pen of a Victorian village blacksmith. I give it here, in its entirety, for the first time:–

There was a time when the gipsies' children would play with the village children. There came a time when they were afraid to meet the old Queen of the Gipsies in the daytime. She was known as Mother Lee, and yet on their carts was the inscription, Liberty Smith, Godshill, Hants. Another inscription read, 'Charity Lee, Odstock'. They had ten children, very fine and of healthy appearance. Their hair was jet black, the same as that of their parents. The old man used to oil and curl his hair, which hung several inches down his back. Especially on Sundays, he dressed in a smock and Top hat, a yellow muffler around his neck. He would go to Church, and he never left the Vicarage empty-handed.

In the afternoons, the children of the villages around would pay visits to the gipsies' Camp, which was known as Joshua's Camp. It was named this in 1800. Later in this story I will explain why it was given this name.

I have watched the children sit and listen to the old woman's tales, and about four o'clock in the afternoon the old woman would say,

'Now my dears, you must go home and have your tea, and come back to school this evening and bring me a bit of tea or sugar or a bit of barley bannock or a few potatoes. You must bring something.'

There was another family, with the name of Joshua Scamp, who used the same Camp. If he had not used this camp it would not have been named Joshua's Camp. Joshua had one son and two daughters. His oldest daughter was often seen with a young gypsy, whose name was Noah Lee, but he appeared before the magistrates and was sentenced for night poaching in Odstock Copse in the name of Noah Cooper. The magistrate asked him his proper name, and he said his mother's name was Cooper and his father's name was Joe Lee. They asked him his age also.

'About eighteen, sir,' was his reply.

. . . There was a terrible case, of which Noah Lee was the cause of all the unpleasant happenings. Every year the farmers hired the gypsies in the spring to destroy the thistles, turnip-hoeing and to pull docks from the corn. Last of all, to cut and tie the corn, sometimes using hooks and sometimes scythes. When the harvest was ended, they were paid their Harvest Money and had a nice supper and a very lively time afterwards. Plenty of cider and home-brewed ale was consumed. Old Gypsy Lee would play the old

Fiddle, and his daughter the Tamboreen. The same instruments they used at their Fatal Wedding, which I will come to later.

The day after the Harvest Supper they would pack up. One half went to Farnbrough and the other half to Kent, picking hops. They always returned to Salisbury Fair, about the middle of October. They were fairly rich when they came. They visited the old beer house and spent a good bit of their Harvest Money. If they took their children, the landlord would not allow them inside, so the gipsies brought their own mugs and basins and were served through the windows. The beer house is called the Yew Tree Inn, and the landlord's name is Bracher . . .

I have already told you Joshua's daughter was often seen with Gypsy Lee, the man with two names. Eventually they got married. Several of the villagers were invited to the wedding – the carpenter, the blacksmith and the sexton as well. On many occasions in the old public house they laughed and talked about this ceremony.

The bride and bridegroom take each other's hands. The fathers-in-laws, they cross hands – Joshua Scamp, the bride's father, and Joseph Lee, the bridegroom's father. It is decided before the clock strikes twelve they are man and wife as long as they live. (This was not a very long life.) They were eating and drinking, playing and dancing, until twelve o'clock, around a large camp fire in the old Clump. The newly married couple went to the Chalk Pit, where a new tent had been erected for the occasion.

They had been married about five months when Old Mother Lee missed some of her tinware, which she used to hawk from door to door . . . She told the Blacksmith she will put evil luck on the person that stole it. She asked him to lend her a looking-glass, which he did. Then she remarked, 'I shall find the thief and my lost tinware', which she did at Noah Lee's Camp in the Chalk Pit.

Noah worked the villages with ware, potato nets, clothes' pegs, etc. He owned some good dogs, ferrets and nets. He was warned from off the camps on the Earl of Radnor's estate.

He went to the New Forest Gypsies' Camp near Godshill. He came to Odstock to see his Father-in-law, Joshua, one Sunday, and he stole the old man's velveteen coat with large brass buttons on it. Joshua had bought this in Salisbury.

Noah told his wife one evening he was going to Southampton, but he took his pony, taking Joshua's coat to ride on. He went to South Newton instead, a few miles out of Salisbury . . .

He arrived at the Beer House and enquired the way to Warminster. He returned to his wife two days later and took her to Romsey.

Old Joshua missed his coat, and he blamed another camp follower by the name of Jack Bachelor. There were two brothers, the other one was Bob. They were very much alike, and they were not guilty of doing any man out of a hard day's work. They were very big men – over six foot in height. They were from thirty to thirty-five years of age. They would fight or wrestle and were good at single-sticks, and have won many a good cheap drink at any of the games. They had a good many meals and shelter under Joshua's tent.

Jack Bachelor was questioned by Joshua about the missing coat, but it was a serious mistake, and this caused a free fight among the gypsies. There was not any gypsy who could beat the Bachelors at that Camp, but later on in the week two men came from Idmiston Camp. Their names were Jack Bull and Nelson Lee. A fight was arranged and took place in the Chalk Pit. Many of the villagers witnessed it.

Just a pair of trousers only they were wearing. Bull was the winner against Bob Bachelor. Then came Nelson Lee against Jack Bachelor. Nelson was winning, but Bob Bachelor struck him unconscious. The gypsies shouted, 'Two to one isn't fair.' There was a heap of stones nearby, and the gypsies old and young pelted the brothers until they begged for mercy. They were a little quieter after this and were not allowed in either of the Odstock Camps. The villagers, even to the little children, were glad to know the big bully brothers were taken down a notch, but it did not finish there. It was years afterwards when they had their last fight.

We now go back to Joshua and the coat. Joshua was a better-class gypsy – very quiet, especially after the death of his wife. A pity his daughter had not died instead . . .

The gypsy children used to come to the Forge. I must tell you about these children. The blacksmith had a pair of tongs, with round flat jaws. He would get them hot. The gypsies would bring a quantity of barley and wheat meal and mix it with water. Sometimes the blacksmith would give them a few currants and a bit of sugar. They put a tablespoonful of dough between these tongs. The blacksmith squeezed the handles together, holding them for a few seconds, open the tongs and out fell the biscuits ready cooked. They called them Pat-a-cakes. The blacksmith often felt sorry that he had showed them how to make these cakes, as they often worried him when he was very busy.

We come to the morning when Joshua's second daughter, eighteen years old, was at the Forge waiting for her donkey to be shod. The old donkey was nearly finished when a strange man came to the shop as a pedlar, selling boot-laces. He also had a few rabbit-skins on his back. Joshua's daughter looked at him very hard when he was leaving the shop. She spoke her father's death sentence. She said,

'Father, that man is wearing your coat which you lost.'

Old Joshua was sharpening his knife on the grinding-stone. He asked the man,

'How did you come by that coat?'

The answer was,

'I got it from a man in Salisbury. I can shew you the man if you will come to Salisbury with me.'

Joshua, thinking that this would be Bachelor, the thief, went with the donkey and cart, the pedlar walking at his side. He asked Joshua to let his daughter come as well, as a witness.

When they got to Salisbury he told Joshua he would report the matter to the super of the Police Force. When they entered the Police Station he told the super that Joshua owned the coat. The super asked Joshua whether he was certain that it was his property.

'Yes, sir, I can tell you how certain marks came here and there.'

'Then I must make you a prisoner.'

Joshua was charged with stealing a valuable cart horse at South Newton. Poor Nellie took the donkey and cart home but left her Father behind. She had not been wanted as a witness; she was wanted to bring back the donkey. The Pedlar was a Policeman in disguise.

The night the horse had been stolen Joshua had not left the Camp. When the trial came on there were several witnesses who swore on oath that Joshua was in Camp at ten p.m., and that a man with a pony and cart horse was seen near Wilton at 10.30, and that it was impossible for any man to go eleven miles in half an hour. Joshua's coat had been left in the stable at South Newton where the coat was stolen. But the truth came to light when it was too late. People never believed that Joshua was guilty, and the village seemed doomed for years afterwards.

The case lasted but three hours. Joshua was sentenced to death and hanged in public, and I amongst thousands of others will not forget the terrible scene.

The name of the Governor of the Prison was Dowding. The coffin was made at Odstock by a carpenter by the name of Bracher. Joshua saw his coffin and said it would do.

When he was on the scaffold he asked for the cap to be removed. This was granted, as he wished to see his friends once more. It was awful to see and hear the screams and shoutings. There was fighting all the way down Fisherton to the Market Square in Salisbury. All the beer houses were closed for several hours.

At Odstock that night there was a dim light in poor old Joshua's Camp. The grave was dug at the south side of Odstock churchyard. There were hundreds of people at the funeral. They disappeared very quietly the next day. Joshua's younger daughter, Nellie, and her brother Tom went to Woodgreen Camp. The old Queen of the Gypsies was in hospital with a fractured leg at the time . . .

Joshua's son-in-law Noah was not at the execution or the funeral. The same year there was a considerable lot of horse and sheep stealing going on. Sheep and deer were often rushed to Whiteparish Hill, and a Southampton man would be there to receive the bootleg.

One Sunday morning a chestnut hunter was missing from a farm near the New Forest. This horse was traced to a place about three miles from Winchester. There were several horses turned out in a pasture for the season, and several chestnuts amongst them. The stolen horse had a long tail and a silver mane, which had been cut off. However, when the owner went to the pasture and called to his mare, of course she came, although he was sixty yards away. They left her there but kept a sharp look-out.

A man was seen driving by daily and looking very hard at the horses. This man resided at Brook Street, Winchester. They got to know where he lived and the beer house he used. Two men went into the beer house one Sunday evening. Each of them had a horse whip. They got into conversation with the man and treated him to a quantity of beer. They were supposed to be horse dealers who were going to Reading that night. They had plenty of money and, flashing a hand full of gold, said they were prepared to buy twenty horses and pay for them at the same time. The man asked how much they would give for a Hunter five years old.

'We must see it first.'

He said, 'Yes. Come with me.'

They were soon on their way through Kingsworthy. One man stayed with the pony; the other caught the Hunter. They were all back in Winchester by half-past nine.

'How much do you want for the Hunter?'

'Twenty pounds.'

'How did you get this mare?'

The answer was not very satisfactory.

'What is your name?'

'Noah Lee.'

'Yes, we know. And we are Police Constables, and we intend to charge you with stealing this horse.'

He was wanted for theft in another county as well, and for stealing two ponies. The trial came on. He was found guilty and hanged.

His wife had a baby at the time, and she told the Police everything concerning her Father's death. The curse of the old Gypsy Queen who had cursed them for stealing her tinware had come true. She said that when she had visited her Father in the condemned cell he had taken her hand and said,

'Mary, I am seventy-one years old and my time is short.

Your husband, Noah, is not yet twenty-one and he may have a long life before him, but he must be very careful. I believe he stole my coat and left it at South Newton.'

She used to say,

'If my Father had told me to divulge the secret I would have done so, but he begged me not to do so. The night that Noah went out and told me he would not return till the morning he did take my Father's coat, and a halter for the horse. The day my Father was executed we stayed in the New Forest. I told Noah then he would suffer some day or other.'

When the people of the towns and villages heard of Noah's arrest and sentence, they were not at all surprised. Not only gypsies but other people visited the grave of Joshua at Odstock. Various cards and flowers were placed on the grave. One inscription read, 'Maintain the truth; then execute justice.' Another said, 'He died for me.'

Everyone seemed to sympathise with Joshua's children. Mary often visited Odstock and never went away hungry or penniless. The baby died shortly afterwards and was buried at Odstock. It was a blessing, too. Her brother Tom and sister Nellie went to near Lyndhurst and lived together. They came to visit their Father's grave the Sunday after a very nice headstone had been erected.

The terrible happenings which I now relate occurred some few years afterwards. Some people thought the Vicar and Churchwardens were to blame.

On the anniversary of the funeral the gypsies arrived at Joshua's Camp. On the Saturday previous old Bracher at the Yew Tree Inn would get in an extra stock of beer and cider for them. Flowers of all descriptions were put on his grave on the Sunday morning. Worse, they planted thorns and briars around his grave and a small yew tree at the foot of the grave.

The yew tree grew rapidly and became unsightly. The Vicar informed the gypsies they were to pull it down. This they would not do. So the Easter vestry decided that it had to pull it all up, and this was done by the old Sexton. His name was Hackett. The Vicar's name was Groves. The Churchwarden's name was Hodding, who was a farmer of a thousand acres in Odstock. There is a tableau for all of them in the church.

The son and daughter of Joshua Scamp visited the grave and saw what had happened. The news was soon circulated to the various gypsy camps.

The gypsies arrived in scores on a Sunday morning. The Old Queen led the Army of Romanies to the Churchyard. They were greatly annoyed. They entered the Church and destroyed everything they could find. There were several yew trees in the Churchyard, and they pulled up every one. They cut the bell rope. There was no service that morning. The shouting and cursing were awful.

They went to the Beer House, and Mr Bracher did a wise thing. He upheld their actions; otherwise it would have been a bad thing for him. They sat on the walls and banks and ate and drank till everything was gone. They had plenty of food and drink given them. Among them were the two brothers named Bachelor.

The old King and Queen stood on the gate by the Church and swore what they would do. The old woman removed her bonnet. She put one hand over her eyes and pronounced five curses of bad luck. The first was on the Parson. She took her hand from eyes and clenched both her fists.

'You will not be preaching this time next year.'

To Mr Hodding the farmer she said with a scream,

'Bad luck will follow you. No son of yours shall ever farm your land.'

To the sexton she shouted,

'You shall be found dead before twelve months more.'

That same evening twenty-five special police constables were sworn in. They were each armed with a club stick, and their pay was two shillings and sixpence. Some of them were set to gather small quickthorns and various small shrubs to plant on the grave. When they met at the church gate, among them were prominent the Bachelor brothers. They had turned traitor against the tribes who had befriended them on many occasions.

In the morning in the church the old Queen had happened to drop her shawl. She went along next day to find it and was given it back again. Several constables were still there. One of them gave her a push and locked the church door behind her. This annoyed her very much. She shouted another curse.

'Any person who locks this door will die before the year is out.'

Then she saw the Bachelor brothers and went into a terrible rage. Clenching her fist she said,

'You will die together, very quickly.'

You could hear her screeching in the next village, Nunton.

The gypsies cleared out of their camps in the next few days. Before they left, the King and Queen put a bunch of flowers on Joshua's grave. They also planted geraniums there, given them by a shepherd at Odstock. Before they left the Queen told Mr. Witt, the old blacksmith,

'My wishes will come true before I come here again.'

. . . As the spring came once more, the farmers were not allowed to hire any gypsy. Farmer Hodding did not want to. His heart was broken, and he regretted ever attending that Vestry Meeting. He did get bad luck for the next two seasons. First, his valuable dairy herd of young and middle-aged animals were struck down with anthrax. They were slaughtered and burnt in the pasture near the Avenue. I saw the constable watching them burn day and night for several weeks. The following year his lambs died by the scores. Nearly everyone you met remarked about how the gypsy's curse was working out.

Then came the curse on the Parson. He was stricken ill with a bad throat. He had an impediment in his speech, so that you could not understand what he said. Soon he died.

John Hackett was found dead by the side of the road one morning, before he reached his work in Longford Park.

As the Bachelor brothers stood by the villagers as Special Constables they were allowed to do a bit of farm work.

A party of five men came for the harvesting. They became friendly with the Bachelors. Their camp was on Shoulder of Mutton Down, and they would always go into Salisbury on Saturdays and reach the beer house at Odstock at nine or ten o'clock. One Saturday night the Bachelors got to the beer house an hour before the other men and later went off towards the camp. They were seen by the keeper, whose name was Tillford. Each carried a rush basket. Some of the gypsies had a camp close by, where they had a nice fire. Early in the morning the keeper moved them on, but the Bachelors were never seen again.

No-one ever troubled about them, as they were so undesirable and they had overdrawn their harvest money, but it seems queer that the keeper saw their basket partly burned when he kicked the fire out. They never came back to harvest since.

That was nine years ago (1861). We have a new vicar, farmer and sexton in the village. I often pay a visit to Joshua's grave, as my father and brother are buried close to him. My brother saw the execution, and I was there too. I asked my father to lift me up in his arms, as I could not see . . .

At this point Hiram Witt's narrative ends, but the story of the Odstock Curse does not. Local people have told me that Hiram did not record the full details about Farmer Hodding. After the Curse, his wife bore several sons, all of whom were born dead. A broken man, Farmer Hodding sold up and emigrated to Australia.

About 1924 the downs above Odstock were taken over to be converted into a racing establishment and were cleared to make gallops. One day in 1929 the manager noticed some uneven spots in the turf. Digging, he found two skeletons, side by side. Mr. Feltham recorded:

They were exactly the same size and length. They measured six foot six. The bones were in good preservation, the jawbones sound, the teeth white. The bones were sent to Birmingham to Sir Charles Hyde but were returned and reburied in the place where they were found. The old saying 'What is done in the dark shall come to the light' is true . . .

Local folk were convinced that these were the bones of the Bachelor brothers. They remembered the Curse that the Brothers should die quickly and together and that (although it seems uncertain whether this was part of the original curse) they should not live to see another harvest.

There remains the curse on the church door. It too worked out dramatically. About the year 1900 an Odstock carpenter was employed to make a new pair of gates for the churchyard. One of his contemporaries takes up the story:

While he was working at the gates, the sexton brought up the subject of locking the church door. The carpenter said the Curse was all rubbish and he was not afraid to lock it. The sexton advised him not to, if he wanted to live another year. It was a job to move the bolt, but the carpenter moved it eventually.

This was spring-time. The sexton, who was a very jocular kind of man, used to say, 'Well, only so many months to Christmas and the end of the year' . . .

One morning he heard groaning from the carpenter's cottage. The sexton and the parson broke down the door and found the carpenter very ill in bed. The doctor sent him to hospital.

When we visited him a fortnight later he said he was nearly ready to come home. But the doctor said he could not do much for him and sent him to another hospital at Bournemouth. He was there for nearly three weeks. His dinner was handed to him. He said,

'I shall get so fat in here my people will not know me when I go home.'

But he never ate that dinner. He died suddenly. His coffin was made on the same premises as Joshua Scamp's. He was buried between the gates that he made and the Church Door . . .

In the 1930s the then rector of Odstock had to go abroad for six months for his health. In his absence, his locum, laughing at the nonsense of the Curse, locked the church door. He died within a year.

The rector, when he returned, threw the key into the river Ebble, where presumably it still lies. The church door at Odstock is never locked.

When last I visited Odstock churchyard a briar rose in bloom was twining itself around Joshua's tombstone. The radio play I wrote attracted much attention locally and apparently resulted in a considerable augmentation of the Odstock church congregation for a few Sundays! An old lady from an Old People's Home in Salisbury walked the two miles over the downs to put a posy of flowers on Joshua's grave.

'I think he deserved it,' she said. 'Don't you?'

11   The Poachers

WHAT REMAINS OF Cranborne Chase is mostly in Dorset, but
originally it was a vast area subject to the usual mediaeval
game preservation laws, and it overlapped considerably into
Wiltshire. King John built a hunting lodge at Tollard Royal.
The northern boundaries of the Chase were in those times
held to be somewhere along the Nadder, from Shaftesbury to
Salisbury, Harnham Bridge being a kind of frontier post. A
fortnight before Midsummer Day a stag's head was mounted
on the bridge. During the period when the hinds were
dropping their calves, known as the Fence Month, every
waggon crossing the bridge had to pay a toll of fourpence and
every pack-horse a penny, as compensation for any
disturbance they might have caused.

During the Middle Ages the Chase belonged at times to the
Crown, at times to the Earls of Gloucester. Although the
rights claimed by the Chase caused frequent friction, real
trouble began when James I granted the Chase to the Earl of

Salisbury. The Earl tried to enforce what he understood to be the ancient privileges and stirred up a hornet's nest. The source of the difficulties was that over the years other landowners had acquired estates within the ancient boundaries of the Chase, notably in the Ebble and Nadder valleys, and what the Earl proposed involved galloping after deer over his neighbours' land. Naturally they objected.

The last attempt to exercise the old rights was made by Lord Rivers, who held Cranborne Chase in the early nineteenth century. With the typical arrogance of the gentry of that period he ordered farmers and estate owners for miles around to pull down their fences, and he gave his keepers instructions to shoot all trespasssing dogs. He even went hunting in Wardour Park, without the permission of its owner. At last a court case was brought by a farmer of Alvediston, whose dog had been shot by a keeper while it was walking quietly with its master. The farmer won, and the long war ended.

Before that, however, generations of young bloods in south Wiltshire and north Dorset found sport in conducting poaching wars in Cranborne Chase. The game was to kill a deer without being caught by keepers. If the keepers intervened, however, so much the better. That would mean a pitched battle, which these young hot-heads enjoyed.

The young squires collected bands of retainers from the local farmers and labourers, and the keepers took to going about in groups, for protection, so sometimes considerable numbers of men were involved. Both sides evolved a kind of armour, examples of which were collected by General Augustus Pitt-Rivers and stored in Farnham Museum. It consists of a long canvas coat, thickly padded with wool, and helmets of plaited straw. For weapons they had quarter-staves and short swords. The maximum fine for anyone caught and convicted was £30, which presented no hardship to the wealthy young landowners and farmers involved.

The situation changed in the reign of George II, when stiffer penalties were enacted. Prison was the penalty for a flagrant offence, and anyone caught twice was given seven years' transportation. This had the effect of checking poaching for sport, at least for a time, but did nothing to deter the village labourers and smallholders, who poached for the pot.

Bowerchalke has a number of stories about local poachers.

One concerns an old lady who, when her cottage was unexpectedly visited by keepers, saved the day by sitting on the iron pot in which the venison was cooking. A place there known as Shepherds' Cross is supposed to mark the spot where shepherds hanged for deer poaching had their bodies displayed in gibbets.

The following accounts, taken from a book entitled *Anecdotes and History of Cranbourn Chase,* written by one William Chafin and published in 1818, are typical of what went on during the poaching war. The incidents are selected from those which occurred on the Wiltshire side of the border.

Another murder, about the same time [1738], was perpetrated in Lord Pembroke's Walk, at Fernditch. One of his keepers was found dead, having been beaten in a most cruel manner with sticks or staves. One criminal alone was detected, although it was not doubted but many were accessory to the murder. This man, whose name was Wheeler, was arraigned and tried at Salisbury, found guilty, and condemned to be hung in chains near the spot where the murder was committed; which sentence was duly carried out. But, in the course of a few nights after, the gibbet was cut down, and the body carried away and thrown into a very deep well at some distance from the place. The weight of the irons carried it to the bottom, and it was not discovered till a long time after . . .

In the year 1791 a villainous set of deer-stealers infested the Chase, particularly Rushmore Walk, and had the audacity to course and kill many deer in an inclosure close to the Lodge. Having been thus successful, the keepers suspected they would repeat their depredations; and therefore, at a particular time when the weather and other circumstances were inviting to the deer-stealers, and the keepers expected them, ten of them from different Lodges assembled singly in the daytime, and concealed themselves in the offices of the mansion, where they remained until night approached, when the first alarm given was the crash of one of the sash windows in one of the rooms on the ground floor. One of the keepers who was nearest to the place immediately sallied forth, and saw a man in the act of cutting a deer's throat, which he had just drawn from the window, through which it had been forced by a dog. The keeper struck the man on the head with his staff just as he was rising from the ground, and most unfortunately the man's cap (which was made of straw, after the manner of bee-pots), gave way, and the point of the staff came into contact with the temple and killed him on the spot.

A most desperate engagement immediately ensued between the deer-stealers and the keepers, exactly even in number, each party ten; the keepers armed with staves and hangers, the enemy with swindgels . . . Many wounds were given and received on both sides; when the keepers, being greatly oppressed by the enemies' weapons, made use of a successful finesse, by gradually retreating into a plantation near the Lodge, where the swindgels could not be made use of; and the keepers with their hangers made such havock, that the whole party were soon defeated, and some took to flight; others, who were badly wounded, surrendered. They were committed to the gaol at Salisbury, tried there, found guilty and transported for life.

The details of the trap sprung by the keepers seem somewhat obscure, but the narrative illustrates accurately the sort of thing that went on. A swindgel, by the way, is a weapon adapted from the threshing flail.

Another tale related by William Chafin concerns a gentleman-poacher who was also a musician. He seems to have resided near Winterslow, though his encounter with Cranborne Chase keepers occurred in Fernditch Walk. Chafin begins by describing how his hero acquired a trumpet.

Having a small quantity of Family Plate, which had adorned his little sideboard for many years and which appeared to him to be in that state useless; after much reasoning with the good lady his Wife, and much persuasion, he obtained her consent to convert it to a better use and to have it converted into musical instruments, which would give them entertainment every day instead of lying dormant on the table. The consent was given with great reluctance, but it was given, and the Husband carried away the plate to London, where he had the whole formed into one instrument, which was a Trumpet . . .

In due course he went poaching in Cranborne Chase.

On a certain favourable night their Leader with his Band of Hunters sallied forth to their sport in Fernditch Walk, where they had met with some success. They were retiring with their prey when the Keepers discovered and pursued them. As the Hunters were encumbered with the spoil, which they did not chuse to abandon, their enemies soon gained ground upon them. The Leader commanded the Band to halt, and, after taken out his silver instrument from its concealment under his Jack (the quilted coat) and thrown a luminous veil, brought from London also, over his cap, he faced and marched alone towards the enemy; who, being struck with the sight and hesitating how to act, made a momentary halt, when our Leader rushed on with quick steps with his silver instrument in his hand, which he presented to their face and gave them what he called a 'flata ta tong'. On which they immediately took to their heels, for they had never heard the sound of a trumpet before, crying out, 'The Devil is after us!'

The same Devil did pursue them and gave a few more blasts from his trumpet before he returned to his associates and assisted in carrying home the venison . . . '

An incidental piece of information provided by Chafin is that 'there is a venerable old wych-elm tree near the gate called Alarm Gate, on the Chase side of it, under which Lord Arundell, the present possessor of Tollard Royal, holds a Court annually, on the first Monday in the month of September.'

Apparently at this Court each keeper had to present a report on the number of deer killed on his beat during the year, together with details of how they were killed and what happened to the carcase. One very old keeper is reported to have said, after the Court had closed for the day, that 'he had taken the old oath, as he had done for three-score following years; but that he must not mind that, for he could have no peace nor content at home unless he made his old Jane's frying-pan hiss now and then; for she could not live without venison, having been so long used to it'.

12　Animals, Plants and Traditional Remedies

IN CHAPTER 9 WE NOTED some of the more spectacular beasts that haunt the Wiltshire countryside. Black dogs are particularly frequent, and there are spectral pigs, donkeys, horses and other creatures. Wiltshire also has its share of tales about witches riding horses at night, and of carters and grooms finding horses lathered with sweat in the morning. These stories, no doubt, relate to smuggling days. Smugglers were in the habit of 'borrowing' any horses they happened to need, and a wise owner would 'turn his face to the wall' when he heard sounds of their nocturnal activities. The witches were as much of an alibi as the moon in the pond at Bishops Cannings.

We have mentioned, too, the propensity of certain witches to turn themselves into hares. Hares were apparently sacred animals in ancient Britain, and folk memory may have retained some of the former beliefs in the guise of superstition. Old Wiltshire villagers used to think it unlucky for a hare to cross their path. When a great-uncle of mine, who had been a notorious poacher, was confined to his house in his old age, shortly before his death he was visited indoors by a hare. This was held to have some significance, and certainly it is unusual for a hare to venture into a house.

Hares, like cats, were called 'pusses', and some country stories revolve around amusing errors that have arisen through confusion of the two. My father used to tell one about an acquisitive resident who saw a well-known poacher apparently stalking a hare across some distant fields. Later he met the man, carrying something in a sack, in the village street. He asked what was in the sack and was told, 'A puss, of course'. He offered half-a-crown for it; then asked to be allowed to see it. 'What? Here in the middle of the street?' exclaimed the poacher, and the buyer saw the force of the argument. So he paid his half-a-crown and took the bag home. Inside was a ginger cat.

The cock is a very usual subject of folk belief, but one such noted in south-west Wiltshire in 1898 is unusual. Generally cocks crowing after dusk are disliked, but around Hill Deverill it was apparently accepted that they would do so, regularly on the hour, right through the night. They would also crow the number of the hour.

The insignificant shrew is also the subject of much folklore. Among old Wiltshire villagers it was commonly known as the 'over-runner', owing to its alleged but fictitious habit of bewitching cows by running over them. Many villages had shrew ashes, as did Gilbert White's Selborne. These were ash trees with holes bored in the trunks and a live shrew sealed inside. Twigs of such trees, applied gently to the affected limbs, were held to be efficacious in the treatment of rheumatism and similar ailments.

Hedgehogs were accused of sucking milk from cows lying in fields. I have also heard the tale about hedgehogs invading orchards and carrying off apples on their spines, though whether that was genuine folklore or a bit of misinformation gleaned from a children's book I cannot say.

An animal less frequently associated than some with witches is the greyhound, but a witch at Potterne is said to have turned herself into a greyhound whenever she wished.

Her story is recorded in the *Wiltshire Archaeological Magazine* (Vol. 50, 1943):

A man was engaged to a young woman living at Potterne, and he made it a habit to walk there and see her most evenings when his work was done, and they used to go for a stroll together. He told me that whenever they went out her mother changed herself into a greyhound and followed them. As a proof of this, he said that on one occasion, when the rain was falling and he and his girl were walking homeward, the greyhound dashed in front of them and leaping the garden gate vanished out of sight. After saying 'goodbye', he walked with his girl up to the house and on looking through the window saw the mother standing in a shallow bath washing mud from her legs.

A Wiltshire animal story which has nothing to do with ghosts or the supernatural but is worth recounting is that of the Winterslow lioness. One October night in 1816 a travelling menagerie was parked at the Pheasant Inn, then known as the Winterslow Hut, on the main London road to Salisbury, in the valley below Winterslow. As the Exeter mail drew up, one of the leading horses was pounced on by a lioness who, unknown to the keepers, had escaped from the menagerie. In the panic that followed, the passengers ran into the inn and barred the door; the coachman and guard remained where they were, though the guard tried to shoot the lioness with his blunderbuss; and a Newfoundland dog grabbed the lioness by a leg but was forced to retire, considerably the worse for the encounter. The dog's gallant intervention, however, distracted the lioness' attention from her prey, and she took refuge among the staddle stones supporting a granary nearby. The menagerie proprietor and his assistants, reluctant to lose such a valuable animal, with remarkable courage crept under the granary. There, by the light of candles, according to the *Salisbury & Winchester Journal,* they 'placed a sack on the ground near her and made her lie down upon it; they then tied her four legs, and passed a cord around her mouth, which they secured; in this state they drew her out from under the granary, upon the sack, and then she was lifted and carried by six men into her den in the caravan'.

There were three sequels to this lively encounter. The unfortunate horse, whose name was Pomegranate, was exhibited, with all her wounds, by the menagerie owner at Salisbury Fair next day. One of the passengers had been left outside in the wild rush for the inn, and while he was there, banging at the closed door, the lioness actually brushed against him. The experience was too much for him, and after a few days he had to be admitted to Laverstock asylum, where he spent the remainder of his life, twenty-seven years. Finally, there developed quite a lioness vogue. No doubt the story was related with relish by stage coach passengers arriving in London during the next few weeks. Artists adopted it and produced oil paintings and, particularly, painted trays depicting the scene. Naturally, the Pheasant Inn has collected some of them, for the pleasure of its guests. The one I like best is a large oil-painting of the lioness clawing at the horse. But the background is the courtyard of an inn not at Winterslow but in London! So Winterslow's lioness is still remembered and has taken her place in the folklore of England as well as of Wiltshire.

Another Wiltshire animal still remembered in folklore is a wild boar. Wishford church has a fine marble memorial to Sir Richard Grobham and his wife, Lady Margaret, who purchased the manor in the reign of Elizabeth I. He was an enthusiastic hunter long remembered locally because he slew a huge wild boar which was 'the terror of the neighbourhood'. His sword and helmet were hung in the church to commemorate the event and remained there until at least the beginning of the nineteenth century. The climax of the chase came when the boar was cornered under a tree known as 'The Boar's Tree'. There Sir Richard gave it the coup de grace. But, mortally wounded, the animal managed to swim across the river Wylye and died on the far bank. Ever afterwards the farmer who owned the land on which The Boar's Tree stood had the right to a pook of hay from the meadow on the far side of the river, on which the boar died. In the middle of the past century men were alive who had exercised that right.

Much of the natural history lore that I absorbed from my elders as a boy in Wiltshire seemed to deal with the weather. I learned that moles throw up larger hills when rain is imminent, and that geese congregate and honk. Other signs of rain are toads becoming active; sheep rising early to graze; old cats playing like kittens; cats washing behind their ears; spiders sitting at the entrance of their webs; green woodpeckers calling. Rooks are said to feed in fields near their rookery when rain is coming, but I think this is because they dislike the strong winds which often accompany rain. It is widely believed that pigs can see the wind and know when it is bringing bad weather.

Signs of fine weather are not so numerous, but it is well known that when the weather is set fair swallows and martins fly high, rooks forage far afield, and small spiders spin gossamer.

Long-range weather forecasting has, according to local folklore, a few natural aids.

'If the ash comes out before the oak
We shall surely have a soak;
If the oak comes out before the ash,
Then we'll only have a splash.'

But I cannot remember ever seeing the oak come into leaf first.

Less well known is:

'When the hen doth moult before the cock,
The winter will be as hard as a rock;
If the cock doth moult before the hen,
Winter will not wet your sole's seam.'

Few people these days keep poultry long enough to see them moulting. Nor is it usually possible now to test the truth of the belief that high ant-hills in summer betoken a long, hard winter; for nearly all of the old downs and pastures which held permanent ant-hills have been ploughed.

Ice in November to bear a duck;
Nothing afterwards but slush and muck

is more often true than false. The belief that a black frost is a long one but that a white frost never lasts more than three days is a sound one applied to weather before Christmas; after that it is not so accurate.

Many of the agricultural sayings are based on long

experience. A peck of March dust is worth a king's ransom'
refers to the desirability of dry weather in that month, so that
spring sowing can be done in good time. 'On Candlemas Day
the farm should have half the straw and half the hay' is a
reminder that on Candlemas Day half the hard weather of
winter still lies ahead.

> When the cuckoo sings on an empty bough,
> Keep your hay and sell your cow

implies that the bough is empty of leaves, signifying a late and
backward spring, when cattle food is likely to be scarce.

> A January spring
> Makes February ring,

is another reminder that much severe weather can still lie
ahead at the end of January, but old Wiltshire villages had a
deep distrust of fair weather in January and used to comment,
'Green January; full churchyard'.

'Long in the bed; long in the head' refers to autumn-sown
wheat. The suggestion is that the wheat plant is better for a
long period of germination, and that is probably true, for
when the plant is slow to send up green shoots it is probably
using the time to establish strong root growth.

> From Christmas to May
> Weak cattle decay

is correct, as is the saying, 'In spring hair is worth more than
meat'. No cattle can expect to be fat at the end of a long
winter, but if they have good winter coats and look healthy in
consequence they will soon fatten on the pastures.

'A late spring never deceives' proclaims a self-evident truth.
When in late spring our corn crops were looking none too
flourishing my father used to say,

> A field of oats in May
> Makes a man run away;
> A field of oats in June
> Makes him sing a different tune;
> A field of oats in July
> Makes a farmer jump for joy.

May is often a dry month, when plants make slow growth, but rain is sure to come eventually.

> Dry May and dripping June
> Put all things in tune

carries the same message. A 'dripping June', however, does not help to achieve the load of hay in June which is, according to a Wiltshire proverb, better than two in July.

Predictably, the belief in forty days of rain after a wet St Swithin's Day (15 July) is still widespread in the county. It is known that St Swithin was a local saint – a 9th century bishop of Winchester.

Some of the farming sayings do not seem to correspond to facts. In the days when Shire horses did most of the farm work there was a strong prejudice against horses with four white feet, but I could never see that the colour of a horse's feet had anything to do with the quality of the animal. Another proverb that seems wrong to me is that 'May kittens never make good cats'. I would have thought that spring-time was the best season for any animal to be born, and there has been nothing wrong with many a May kitten we have had. The belief that guinea-fowl keep rats away from a farm would seem to have no foundation whatever, but I can see the point of 'Where a farm keeps geese, the farmer's wife wears the breeches!' Few farmers like having geese on their pastures because they foul the grass, but on old-time farms geese often provided the farmer's wife with pin-money, and a strong-minded woman could overcome her husband's reluctance.

Another local legend about rain comes from Boreham Mill, near Warminster. Beside the mill is a field in which rain always interrupts haymaking; indeed, to cut the grass will always bring on a shower. The trouble arose because one wet summer the farmer turned his 'pooks' (heaps of hay) on a Sunday, the first fine day for a long while. To justify this, he hid his watch under one of the pooks, and, when asked why he was not keeping the Lord's Day, he explained that he had lost his watch and was searching for it. Finally, coming to the last unturned pook, he revealed the watch beneath it and returned home, satisfied. (Sabbath-breaking was much disapproved of in the nineteenth · century. A worker employed by a correspondent of *Folk-Lore,* in which the account appeared in 1900, went fishing on Sunday and caught a 'horful crittur, with terrible heyes fearsome to look at'. The monster was promptly returned to the water, and the man went home convinced that he had met the devil – a punishment for violating God's law. When I was a boy at Pitton I heard of some boys who, many years earlier, went 'scuggy-hunting' (squirrel-hunting) in Clarendon Woods on Sunday afternoon and had been frightened by the devil. No-one would think of gardening, sewing or knitting on a Sunday, and only religious papers were permitted in most houses.

Much weather lore is concerned with the moon. Even now many countrymen will swear that the weather changes when the new moon appears. When a new moon is seen with its horns upwards, saucer-like, it is said that 'the moon is holding water'; a wet month lies ahead. The moon is also supposed to govern the wind, and the wind controls the water level in wells. After long spells of south-western weather, the wells fill.

Until quite recently the moon controlled many rural activities. Seeds had to be sown when the moon was waxing, so that as the moon increased so would they. Oddly, there was an exception; for some unknown reason, beans and peas had to be sown when the moon was waning. Fat beasts had also to be killed when the moon was waxing; otherwise their meat would go bad as the moon declined.

The moon was held to affect human behaviour, and modern science is investigating this belief. My father used to tell me, laughing, how my maternal grandmother would walk through the woods on a moonlit night with a parasol over her head, to ward off the moonbeams. He thought it absurd, but she was observing an old notion that moonbeams could harm her in some way, even if only to the extent of spoiling her complexion.

Even now many of us will turn our money when first we see a new moon; and we believe it unlucky to see the new moon through glass. Not long ago I heard of an elderly lady who went outside to look at the new moon, because she refused to see it through the window. But she kept her glasses on!

Which brings us to the matter of luck, regarded very seriously by our ancestors. It was widely believed that certain people attracted good luck and others bad luck, though bad luck could often be averted by taking the proper magical precautions, such as the still common one of throwing spilt salt over the left shoulder. More realistic is the farming proverb, 'Muck is luck', implying that the farmer who manages his land well and puts plenty of muck on it does not need to rely on luck.

Magpies are harbingers of luck, good or bad, but there seems to be some doubt about which. The version I have most frequently heard is,

> One for sorrow,
> Two for mirth,
> Three for a wedding,
> Four for a birth.

Another variant says it is lucky to see a single magpie but unlucky to see more.

A lullaby, noted about a hundred years ago, shows clear dislike of the species:

> Hush-a-bye, babby,
> The beggar shan't have 'ee,
> No more shall the maggotty-pie (magpie)
> The rook nor the raven
> Shan't car' (carry) thee to heaven
> So hush-a-bye, babby, by-bye.

It is extremely unlucky to kill a robin or a swallow, and when I was a boy we were assured that anyone who robbed a robin's nest would have a crooked finger. For martins or swallows to nest on or in a building was very lucky. As children we knew the rhyme,

> The robin and the wren
> Are God's cock and hen.

On the other hand, for a robin to enter a house was unlucky, especially if a person were lying sick. It betokened death. Nor, apparently, was it desirable *not* to hear the cuckoo at the right time. If anyone failed to hear it by Warminster Fair, he was told: 'You must go to Warminster Fair and buy one'. The Fair was held on 23 April.

A bumble-bee coming indoors indicated the arrival of a friend, but rats and mice entering the house of a sick person showed that death was imminent. If your nose itches you will be 'kissed, cursed or vexed'. If your left hand itches, money will be leaving you; if your right hand, you will soon receive money. Your ears burning signify that someone is talking about you; if it is the right ear they are praising you; if the left, they are criticising. My small Wiltshire grandchildren know how to tell fortunes by the white marks on the nails of their right hand, just as we did when children. One reads from thumb to little finger, chanting, 'A gift; a friend; a foe; a lover; a journey to go.'.

Another belief about travelling concerned any child with a 'double crown' on his head – that is, two points from which the hair radiates. This showed that he would 'eat his bread in two portions'.

A whole series of rhymes is attached to the plumstones on the side of one's plate at the end of dinner. They are counted to foretell the future, or, in the case of girls, the occupation of their future husband. The best known is, of course, 'Tinker, tailor, Soldier, sailor, Rich man, poor man, Beggarman; thief.' The girls would try to discover when they were going to be married – 'This year; next year; sometime; never'; What they would wear – 'Silk, satin, muslin, rags'; how they would ride to church – 'Coach, carriage, wheelbarrow, dungcart'; and where they would live – 'House, cottage, pigsty, barn.'

Girls would also try to pare an apple without breaking the peel, which they would then wave three times around their head and throw over their left shoulder. As it fell it would form the initial of their true love.

Mothers would never cut the nails of a child under one year, and even now I sometimes see mothers biting the nails of their small children. Nail parings in the old days were carefully collected and burnt, lest witches should get hold of them and use them for spells. Hair was treated the same way after trimming, lest a frog should spit on it, which was considered extremely unlucky.

After childbirth a mother should always go upstairs before she went down, or the child would not prosper. Sometimes steps were brought for her to use. It was lucky to fall upstairs but unlucky to pass someone on the stairs.

> When wood refuses to kindle fire,
> Something comes that we desire

seems to be a kind of consolation for an exasperating state of affairs. I once met an old man who said he used to kindle his cottage fire by means of tinder and flint. It used to take him twenty minutes or so in the morning to get a fire started. However, an old saying asserts that it is unlucky to find a hearth fire alight in the morning. It is also unlucky to leave supper on the table overnight.

If on getting up in the morning you put your clothes on inside out you will have good luck – that is, if you do it by mistake. A good housewife will open all her windows wide to let the New Year in. She will never turn a bed on Friday or Saturday, as that will bring bad luck. My mother used to recite a rhyme, most of which I have forgotten, about the luck which attends housewives who do their washing on the various days of the week. I remember that the last two lines are:

> They that wash on Friday, wash in need;
> And they that wash on Saturday are dirty sluts indeed.

Never accept a knife or scissors without giving something in return. Be careful about buying the clothes of a dead person, as they wear out quickly. Never sit in a chair immediately it has been vacated by an old person, or you 'will follow that person to the grave as quickly'. Bad luck comes in triplicate; if you break one thing you will certainly break three. I have known housewives deliberately break an old saucer or something of little value, after having broken two things by accident, so that the sequence can be completed and the run of bad luck ended. According to one version, the unused part of an onion should never be kept in a house, as it will 'breed sickness'. Another version says exactly the opposite.

No old-time cottager would burn elder wood indoors. Elder is a witches' tree and is also said to attract snakes. Another witches' tree is holly. Even now, with the reason all but forgotten, workmen trimming hedges, although they may be using a mechanical hedgecutter, will usually leave holly trees untouched, standing above the level of the hedge. But it seems that, basically, holly is good magic, and so lucky, whereas elder is bad magic. Elder will attract witches, holly will keep them at bay.

Willow should always be chopped or cleft. It is considered very unlucky to saw it, and particularly so to bring willow logs indoors for burning. Hawthorn, on the other hand, is a good-omened tree. Village maypoles were usually of hawthorn. A sprig of it over a cowshed is said to ensure good milking.

People at Manor Farm, Hill Deverill, thought that if a branch was blown off certain old ash trees nearby, a member of the family was going to die. This was recorded in 1889.

Sycamores have slightly unlucky associations, perhaps because they were also sometimes known as 'hanging trees'. This was perhaps because they generally have a horizontal branch or two at a convenient height for hanging a man. I have heard that sycamores were once planted at mile intervals along the old Shaftesbury Drove, which is the ancient hill road linking Salisbury with Shaftesbury, but whether these had anything to do with facilities for hanging highwaymen and other rogues I cannot say.

Many old cottages have periwinkles along the garden banks. These were often planted when a newly-married couple took possession of the cottage, in the belief that the periwinkles would ensure a lucky and happy marriage.

Among the lowlier plants used by witches for various purposes, whether good or bad, were yarrow – very potent in the casting of spells – parsley, nightshade, devil's bit scabious – common on the Wiltshire downs – St John's wort and thyme. Kathleen Wiltshire records that along a lane at Bishops Cannings, known as Pig Lane, a passerby may occasionally get two whiffs – never more – of the scent of thyme. This is said to denote that a murder was at some time committed there.

She also mentions that on high Winklebury Hill, in the south-western corner of the county, a hawthorn marks the site of an earlier thorn known as The Witches' Scrag Tree – a trap for witches coasting low over the hill on their broomsticks. 'It is said that at the time of the full moon a spate of them would littter the hill with their corpses'

The present tree was, I believe, planted by the villagers of Berwick St John at some time since the first world war. The party joined hands and danced around it, singing 'Blessing

164 Animals, Plants and Traditional Remedies

and peace to Berwick St John'. A bonfire was lighted, and then an imaginary witch was discovered in some tree branches and was duly burned!

The curious legends surrounding the mandrake seem to have been derived from the shape of its root. The true mandrake of Mediterranean countries is not found in England, and so the traditions have become attached to the root of the white bryony. This is a large tuberous root, of the yam family, which often bears a superficial resemblance to a crude human figure, cleft at the end to represent legs. Digging up mandrakes was considered highly dangerous, for at the moment of extraction the root, or the demon which possessed it, was said to let out such an unearthly shriek that anyone hearing it would drop dead. A correspondent of *Folk-Lore*, Monica Money-Kyrle, who lived at Whetham, near Calne, showed a mandrake root from her garden to the local Women's Institute members. One old lady then recounted how her husband had dug one up, to show her that there was nothing to be feared in doing so, but shortly after this he had died. The root has an intensely bitter taste. Potions prepared from it were an aphrodisiac and were also supposed to cure insomnia and constipation.

A tremendous amount of folklore attaches to the cure of warts. A few years ago I invited readers of my weekly column in the *Western Gazette* to share with me their favourite wart cures, and, although responses came from all over Wessex, I found on enquiry that most of the remedies were known in Wiltshire.

One group of cures is herbal. It is said that one can rub on the warts the juice of the greater celandine; the juice of dandelion flower stems; the juice of an elder stem 'on which the sun has not shone'; the juice of heliotrope leaves, mixed with salt; the juice from the leaves or branches of a fig tree; the soft, downy material found inside broad bean pods; hart's tongue fern, bruised; the juice of leek; of milk thistles; of St John's-wort; of petty spurge; of white mullein; wheat leaves, mixed with salt; garden rue, or wild thyme, boiled in urine with pepper and nitre; the roots of teazel, boiled in urine and made into an ointment; the burnt ashes of willow bark, mixed with vinegar.

Then there are substances from the chemist's shop or the domestic larder. These include castor oil, or washing soda rubbed on; a mustard plaster; a two-percent solution of arsenic; mother of pearl buttons, dissolved in lemon juice and used as an ointment.

A very hot pin, stuck deep into the centre of the wart, sounds a painful cure. Much more pleasant to 'drink only fresh water from springs'. To cover with a cobweb, which is afterwards burned, does not sound very hygienic, but a sheet cobweb was an old remedy for a number of ailments, particularly the staunching of bleeding. Many of the wart remedies are pure magic, as, for instance, the following:

> Cut a piece of brown paper, nine inches square. Take the pods of three broad beans and rub the downy inner side vigorously against three separate warts. Lay the pods on brown paper, taking care that they do not touch another surface. Fold the paper to make a neat packet three inches square and tie with a piece of string three feet long. This work must be done in secret, with no-one watching or knowing anything about it. Take the package into a town or village street, drop it and hurry on, without turning round. Choose a position where you can see whether anyone picks it up without being able to identify the person. The warts will then be transferred to that person, provided you will that they will be. And to prove that you really do believe you must not examine your hands for warts for at least nine days.

I would think that the last rule would effectively ruin that remedy.

The principle of passing on the wart underlies several of the magical remedies, as does the notion of secrecy. A wart can be bought by a witch. One girl was sent a penny, carefully wrapped in cotton wool and packed in a match-box. She was told to put the penny in a charity box as soon as the warts disappeared, which they did very shortly. One of my daughters, when a small girl, was told by a local woman to rub raw steak on a wart and then to bury it, secretly, in the garden, without telling anyone about it, and using her fingers to dig the hole. As the steak rotted, the warts would vanish. It seemed to work. One version of this remedy insists that the steak should be stolen, and perhaps my daughter stole her piece of steak from our larder.

Elder can be used instead of steak. Cut a very young elder shoot. Carve on it as many notches as you have warts. Bury, and the warts will disappear as the shoot decays. But if anyone finds it and picks it up, the warts will be transferred to that person. Very similar is the cure which consists of cutting an apple in half, rubbing the two parts over the wart, tying them together again and burying them. As the fruit rots, the warts will vanish.

The blood of certain small animals, especially the mole and the mouse, but also the cat, is said to be effective, if rubbed on the wart. So is fasting spittle, meaning the saliva before one's mouth is rinsed out in the morning. Fasting spittle, incidentally, is also held to be good for weak eyes.

Predictably, there is a moon remedy. 'When there is a full moon, go secretly into the garden and, facing the moon, hold your hands towards it and recite three times, 'Moony, moony, take my warts away'. Say nothing to anyone, and believe that the cure will work.'

What prompted my enquiry into wart cures was that at the time I had a rash of warts on one hand. From all those remedies I collected I selected fourteen, to correspond with the number of warts I had, and decided to try one on each. However, before I got started I visited an old friend in hospital and, by way of conversation, told him what I was doing. He looked at them and told me to go away and forget about them. The warts all disappeared before I had had time to apply the other remedies!

Ash trees, or willows, were commonly used in an old-time cure for rupture. The tree in question had to be a 'maiden' tree – that is, one which had never been pruned or pollarded. A long slit was made in it, two parts forced open, and the ruptured infant passed through. The slit was then tightly bound, and as the tree healed so would the baby. Mrs Wiltshire mentions two old men of Baydon, born as ruptured babies, who were passed through a tree in this way. The tree in this instance was, unusually, a birch.

In the Wiltshire Archeological Magazine, Canon Eddrup, the vicar of Bremhill, mentions an instance of a boy of that parish who, some thirty or so years earlier, had been given this treatment to cure a rupture. The ceremony had to be performed at sunrise on 1 May, and the child had to be passed through the slit ash with his head towards the sun. Another boy, then ten or eleven years old, was similarly treated, but his rupture did not heal. This was attributed by his mother to the fact that the tree had been cut down before the healing was complete.

Canon Eddrup also relates that in 1876 he heard of a local man who claimed to be able to cure 'yaller jarndice' by inspecting the urine of the sick person and 'doing something to it'. He was told that the ashes of a maiden ash tree were used in some way and that the cure could be effected without the healer seeing the sufferer. The gift had been passed down by the father and mother of the healer.

A maiden ash features again is an old Wiltshire cure for neuralgia 'Cut a piece off each finger and toe nail and a piece off your hair. Get up on the next Sunday morning before sunrise and with a gimlet bore a hole in the first maiden ash you come across and put the nails and hair in; then peg the hole up'.

Among herbal 'teas' still in quite common use in Wiltshire are those made from mint, raspberry leaves, camomile and sage. They are used to give relief from colds and other common ailments. My mother used to tell me that when I was a very small child my life had been saved by raspberry tea. I have often had powdered holly berries mixed with lard rubbed on my chilblains. Tallow candles were once rubbed on my chest 'to move the phlegm' after a troublesome cold. Goose grease was perhaps a more widely used remedy for chest ailments and for painful or swollen joints. It was also popular, as a veterinary medicine, for massaging udders. Mullein leaves are said to make a very good poultice. I have also been poulticed with hot, damp bread. Snail broth used to be regarded as a remedy for tuberculosis, or 'consumption' as it was then called. The snails, or black slugs would do, were boiled in milk, strained and served before breakfast.

More superstitious remedies included the hair cut from the cross on a donkey's back, placed in a bag and hung around the sufferer's neck as a cure for whooping cough. The verdigris scraped from church bells and made into an ointment was recommended as a cure for shingles. An alternative was house-leek juice.

To prevent painful attacks of cramp at night, corks should be tied around the limb in which the attack is expected, or they should be placed under the pillow. An alternative was to place a magnet with points facing towards the foot of the bed; better still was a hag-stone under the bed. A hag-stone is a flint with a hole in it. Even today one may occasionally be seen, hanging outside a cottage door to keep away witches.

Most old Wiltshire farmhouses and cottages had bread-ovens, which were usually coffin-shaped orifices built into the masonry of the chimney corner. The method was to place a whole faggot in the oven and allow it to burn to ashes behind the shut door. The oven was hot enough for baking when a 'fire-brick' at the inner end of the oven glowed white-hot. The ashes were then quickly raked out and the loaves put in. It was said that 'if a loaf baked on Good Friday were hung up in the cottage, it would ensure that light bread should be baked all the year through.' Such a safeguard, if effective, would be much appreciated, for bread-ovens were sometimes affected by what appears to have been a fungus infection which produced what was known as 'rimy bread'. The interior of the loaf formed filaments or fibres instead of wholesome bread and had an unpleasant, sour taste. Incidentally, a large hole inside a cottage loaf was unlucky; it signified a grave.

North-west Wiltshire was once a great cheese-making district, and Marlborough was a noted cheese market. Of the problems of cheese-making John Aubrey writes:

> About Lidyard, in those fatt grounds, in hott weather, the best huswives cannot keep their cheese from heaving. The art to keep it from heaving is to putt in cold water. Sowre wood-sere grounds doe yield the best cheese, and such are Cheshire. Bromefield, in the parish of Yatton, is so – sower and wett – and where I had better cheese made then anywhere in all the neighbourhood.

He adds:

> Now of late, about 1680, in North Wiltshire, they have altered their fashion from thinne cheeses about an inch thick, made so for the sake of drying and quick sale, called at London Marleborough cheese, to thick ones, as the Cheshire cheese.

The Rev. A. C. Smith, in the Wiltshire Archaeological

Magazine, records as a Wiltshire proverb,

If you'll have a good cheese, and have'n cold,
You must turn 'n seven times before he's cold.

In the last decade of the nineteenth century, a Wiltshire County Council Cheese School existed at Whitley Farm. Regrettably the technique being taught, known as Mrs Vines' method, did not include the seven turns, recommended by the Rev. Smith. But the eccentric and complex process involved probably produced a good cheese, similar to those made in Gloucestershire at one time. One interesting feature was the addition of a special cheese spice, supplied by Messrs Neale of Chippenham, the proportion being one teacupful to a hundredweight. The finished product was evidently orange-yellow, the same as various modern hard-pressed cheese. Annatto, the normal colouring agent, was used to achieve this; it grows in Central and South America, where it served as a natural dye, and also as a stain for body decoration.

In type, this brand of Wiltshire probably differed little from earlier local cheeses, though by now two varieties, large and small, known as Flat and Loaf Wiltshires, had become more or less standardised. These resulted from slightly different processes, the Flat cheese owing something to the Cheddar system. Records from the mid-19th century mention a third variety, known as a Little Wiltshire, evidently a soft-curd cheese made for quick consumption, and probably rather like a Petit-Suisse.

Factors in Bath were, so it was said in 1798, the major purchasers of north Wiltshire's 5,000 tons annual production. The cheese was considered equal to the Gloucestershire and was 'mostly esteemed by genteel people'. Large loaves of 5 to 12 lb. weight became the usual size, and locals boasted that the curd was 'reduced to atoms' during manufacture – a claim as literally meant as it was surprising. Marlborough had a big cheese market, and merchants there sought out north Wiltshire's best production, for sale to London. Hence it was sometimes known as Marlborough cheese.

But cheese-dealing on a still larger scale went on at Weyhill Fair, a few miles over the border in Hampshire, with records going back to the eleventh century. Hops grown in the south-east were sent across country by waggon for sale there, and Wiltshire cheeses were picked up as a return load. Most of Somerset's Cheddars, as well as the Wiltshire Loaves, were marketed at Weyhill.

North Wiltshire cheese apparently achieved its excellent reputation because the geography of the farms was considered particularly suitable. With a farmhouse in the centre of the farmland 'all the cows can be driven home to milk, and all the milk put together at an even temperature'; moreover, 'by beginning their work early the dairymen can make cheese twice in the day.' In other counties, with farm organization usually based on the milkmaid milking in the pastures, this was not possible.

Cattle in north Wiltshire were mostly Longhorns, and one dairy milked 200 cows at three different houses – a huge herd, by past standards. Farms often produced up to six tons of cheese annually, and a few establishments could even reach 25 tons or more. A good Longhorn would yield $4\frac{1}{2}$-5 cwt., and nearly all could achieve three.

Sheep in Wiltshire were traditionally referred to as 'the golden hoof', for by their manure they made the economic cultivation of the light chalk lands possible. Downland farms were so essentially based on a sheep and corn economy that the Wiltshire proverb, 'All goes to the devil where the shepherd is evil' was strictly accurate. The local breed was the Wiltshire Horn sheep, which has now become rare.

A queer belief is recorded for Tidworth, that larks used their long hind claw to pierce the brain of a sheep and give it the disorder known as 'giddy'. 'That spur on his foot, that be poison,' said one old man.

Sheep-ticks were once swallowed as a remedy for rheumatism, though whether live or cooked is not stated. Spiders were certainly swallowed live for some ailments, and live frogs were a popular remedy for illness in cows. Holes were cut in calves' ears on Good Friday to ward off illness during the coming summer.

An amusing tale is told of a girl, Mary Humby, born in the early eighteenth century at Teffont. As she was the tenth child of the family she was taken to church for baptism with a sprig of myrtle attached to her christening gown, so that the Rector would not be able to claim her as a tithe!

As boys at Pitton we had names, which I have since found are or were widespread in Wiltshire, for many familiar animals, birds and flowers. For some of the commonest we used the diminutive 'ie', as in 'chinkie' for chaffinch; 'greenie' for greenfinch, 'goldie' for goldfinch, 'spadgie' (or sometimes 'spadger') for sparrow, 'hedgie' for hedge-sparrow, 'blackie' for blackbird, and 'drushie' for thrush. Our names for the corn-bunting and the meadow pipit – 'bunt-lark' and 'tit-lark' respectively – apparently derived from our observation that these birds do indeeed resemble larks.

We had no alternative names for the swallow, robin, cuckoo, starling and most of the tits, but the long-tailed tit had two. It was known as the 'bottle-tit', a reference to the shape of its nest, or the 'long-tailed cavy'. Wrens also had two alternative names – 'cutty wren' or 'jinny pooper'. The pied wagtail was the 'polly dishwasher'.

Our 'curlew' was the stone-curlew, then common on the downs, though now becoming very rare. The lapwing was the 'peewit'. Pheasants were familiarly known as 'longtails'. The heron was the 'jack hern', and there was a vulgar belief that the bird was straight-gutted, it being frequently possible to find a countryman who would swear that he had seen a heron swallow the same eel three or four times.

My father had names for two birds now seldom seen in downland Wiltshire but apparently familiar enough in the 1880s and 1890s to have local names. One was the stonechat, which he called the 'blackcap' and which he said was a common visitor to sheep-folds in winter; the other was the now very rare red-backed shrike, which he called the 'high mountain sparrow'. The brambling, which associates with chaffinches in hard winters, is still to Wiltshire villagers as the 'bramble-finch'. Gulls were seldom seen inland in my father's youth, when they did appear they were regarded as harbingers of rough weather.

A mole was a 'want'; a shrew, an 'over-runner'. A newt, commoner when I was a boy than it is now, was an 'evvet', a corruption, no doubt, of the old English word 'eft'. An ant was an 'emmet'. A squirrel was a 'scuggy', and a hare, as noted on page 153, was often referred to as 'puss'.

Among plants, the traveller's joy was 'bithewine', a word which I still find myself using; goose-grass was 'clyder'; chamomile was 'maddern'; knot-grass was 'stone-weed' or 'wire-weed'. Sallow was, of course, 'palm' and was traditionally used for decorations on Palm Sunday and at

Easter. Wild anemones were 'wind-flowers', but our 'cuckoo-flowers' were not the species generally so-called but the greater stitchwort.

We called hips, the fruit of the wild rose, 'cankers', and haws 'hen-eggs'. The fruit or seed of the mallow was 'bread-and-cheese', and we used to eat it. We also used to suck yew-berries, swallowing the soft red pulp and spitting out the green core – a dangerous practice, for the core is highly poisonous.

As children we were familiar with the Bloody-nosed Beetle, a large, slow-moving black beetle which exudes a red fluid from its mouth-parts. We used to spit on it, 'to see it bleed'. To see this beetle moving about was also considered a sign of rain.

Any green caterpillar was a 'palmer' – and I have wondered whether this was a derisory reference to mediaeval pilgrims or palmers, who may well have been regarded by sedentary peasants as a similar pest! Snails were supposed to be particularly numerous on Snail Down, near Everley – hence the name. This is what local people told Professor Thomas in 1953, but investigation showed the area to be poor in molluscs. Perhaps there is really a different explanation, or, since the name is old, there may have been more snails at one time. We used to refer to any small troublesome insect pest as 'blight', though the term was reserved more particularly for aphids. Grey, close, thundery weather was known as 'blighty' weather. The small rove-beetles which abound under such conditions were 'thunderbugs'.

Woodlice were 'barley-buts' – and still are, as far as I am concerned, though I have also heard them called 'granfers' and 'bakers'. A rhyme noted in 1894 made them into 'butchers', and children believed that reciting it caused them to curl up:

> Granfer-grig killed a pig,
>   Hung en up in corner
> Granfer cried and piggy died,
>   And all the fun were over

A bumble-bee is also a 'dumbledore'. A dragonfly was a 'hostinger' – an entire misrepresentation of the dragonfly's habits, as it does *not* sting horses! Moths were sometimes called 'millers'.

Hazel catkins were affectionately known as 'pussycats'. The garden stock was the 'gillyflower'. Wild pansy was 'love nidols', which was probably a corruption of 'love-in-idleness'.

Some of the dialect words we used have an added interest because they refer to farm and domestic activities which are now obsolete. For instance, we 'spleeshed' a hedge, which meant laying it by half-severing the growing bushes just above ground level. The finished interwoven hedge was kept in place by a tightly-woven top layer of supple rods known as 'edders' or 'heathers'. We thatched our ricks and cottage roofs with 'yealms' or 'elums', which are bundles of straw thatch. The straw bonds for tying 'yealms' were twisted with the help of a tool known as a 'wimble' – and many a day have I spent at the job. We stood our sheaves to dry in 'hiles'; our hay was gathered in 'pooks'. We measured our garden plots in 'lugs', equal to a rod, pole or perch, and a cottager could estimate the size of a garden in lugs as accurately as a farmer could judge the size of a field in acres, just by looking at it.

A 'plough-bottle' was a small barrel used for taking the day's ration of cider or ale to the fields. A 'kivver' was a container for bread. We used to sift flour or ashes or soil with a 'rudder' not a sieve, and we called it 'ruddering'. A loft was a 'tallet'; a granary, a 'gurner'. A 'spudgel' was a kind of bucket fixed on the end of a pole for baling water out of ditches or for filling water-barrels.

Farm workers in my youth would refer to 'nammit' for lunch. My father was more precise. He said that 'nammit' referred particularly to a snack, or lunch, taken at nine o'clock. An afternoon snack, at three o'clock, was a 'jewbit'. 'Nammit' could also be used for the first cut from a loaf, for which another name was 'kissy bread'.

Brushwood faggots used for burning in bread-ovens or limekilns were 'bavvins'. Sheep's knuckle-bones were 'dibs', and a game used to be played with them. The mushroom-shaped stones on which ricks or granaries were perched to keep out rats were 'staddles'. Hurdles in sheep-pens were fastened to upright stakes, 'shores', by means of 'shackles'. Threshing-rubbish was 'caven', and raking it away from the threshing-machine was one of the least attractive jobs during threshing operations.

13 Some Wiltshire Songs

I HAVE BEEN TRYING to recall some of the songs I learned at home when I was very young. My mother often sang 'Mother Bond' to me and I remember several verses.

Mrs. Bond, she flew to the pond in a rage,
With her lap full of onions and her hands full of sage,
Crying, Dilly, dilly, dilly, will ee come and be killed?
Crying, Dilly, dilly, dilly, will ee come and be killed?
You ungrateful little creatures, don't I feed you every day?
'Oh yes, Mrs Bond, but we'll all fly away.'
So, quack-quack-quack-quack-quack-quack-quack, Good-bye, Mrs Bond.

Several of the lines were repeated. The word 'dilly' for duck is interesting. We used to refer similarly to 'coopies' for hens, and to 'chookies' for pigs. A cow was a 'dummick'.

Another verse I learned as a boy concerned the miller, who

was apparently an unpopular character in villages in the old days.

> Miller-dee, miller-dee, dusty-pole,
> How many sacks of flour hast thou stole?
> In goes a bushel, out comes a peck,
> Hang old miller-dee up by the neck.

Rather similar was the song about Johnny and the coffee mill.

Johnny grinds the coffee-mill, mixing the sugar with the sand,
Now at the corner pub, 'tis drinks all round he'll stand.
But now he's grinding a different mill, mixing lots of stone,
All through the poor boy mixing his master's money with his own.

Or, to quote an old Wiltshire couplet,

> Him what takes what isn' hissen
> Ull find hisself shut up in prizen.

My mother used to sing a round which I think must be local, because it seems to refer to Salisbury Plain.

> May Day's breaking,
> All the world's awaking,
> Let us see the sun rise over the Plain.
> Why have you awoke me?
> How you do provoke me!
> Let me have a little time to doze off again.
> Sleeping in the daytime,
> Waste the happy Maytime,
> Makes an empty pocket and a cloudy brain.

In the Wiltshire Archaeological Magazine, for 1943, a contribution by H.C.B., in *Moonrake Medley*, records two songs collected from Mr Alfred Lockey, of Bedwyn, who died in 1941. The first is 'We are all Jolly Fellows that follow the Plough' and runs,

> It was early one morning by the break of day.
> The cocks were a-crowing, the farmer did say,

'Come all you bold fellows, come rise with good will,
Your horses want something their bellies to fill.'

When four o'clock comes, then up we do rise
And into the stable, boys, nimbly we flies,
With rubbing and scrubbing our horses, I vow,
We are all jolly fellows that follows the plough.

Then six o'clock comes; to breakfast we meet.
With beef, bread and port we so heartily eat.
With a piece in our pocket, I'll swear and I vow
We are all jolly fellows that follows the plough.

When seven o'clock comes, then to harness we goes —
Hop over the plain, boys, as nimbly as does,
And when we get there we are jolly and bold
To see which of us the straight furrow can hold.

Our master came to us, and this he did say,
'What have you been doing this long summer's day?
You ain't plough one acre, I swear and I vow.
You are all lazy fellows that follows the plough.'

I stepped up to him, and I made this reply,
'We have all ploughed an acre, so you tell a lie.'
Our master turned to us and laughed at the joke:
'It's past two o'clock boys, it's time to unyoke.

Unharness your horses and rub them down well,
And I'll give you a jug of bonny brown ale.'
So ne'er fear your masters. I swear and I vow
We are all jolly fellows that follows the plough.

When singing this song, which he did regularly at local festivals, Mr Lockey would raise his glass of ale and give the following toast:

The inside of a loaf and the outside of a jail,
A pound of beefsteak and a pot of good ale.
Here's to the crow that sits on the plough —
If he ben't got off, he's on there now.

The second of Mr Lockey's songs is only a fragment, as he

could not remember all the verses properly. It is entitled 'The Carter's Lad's Song.'

> Crack, crack, goes my whip,
> I whistle and I sing,
> I sit upon my waggon,
> As happy as a king.

> My horses always willing,
> For me, I'm never sad,
> There's none can lead a happier life
> Than Jim the Carter's lad.

> For it's crack, crack, goes my whip,
> I whistle and I sing,
> I sit upon my waggon,
> I'm as happy as a king.

> I snap my fingers at the snow,
> I whistle at the rain,
> I've braved the storm for many a day
> And can do so again.

The first verse is then repeated as a chorus.

A song known to shepherds in the Bourne valley and eastern parts of Wiltshire when I was a boy was:

> Crafty is the hare, cunning is the fox,
> Why should not this little calf grow up to be an ox?
> To search for his living among the briars and thorns,
> And die like his daddy, with a great pair of horns.

It is a drinking song and was, I believe, used at an initiatory ceremony for shepherds during annual festivities at the great Weyhill Fair. Weyhill is, of course, in Hampshire, though within a few miles of the Wiltshire border, but, as one might expect, the song was well known to Wiltshire shepherds.

14   Local Humour

THE CLASSIC WILTSHIRE STORY, repeated by all who write about the county, is the Wiltshire Moonrakers.

One moonlit night, a couple of centuries or so ago, two men of Bishops Cannings were surprised in the task of dragging a hay-rake through the local pond.

On being asked what they were doing, one replied, 'We be a-reaking for thik thur girt cheese.'

'Cassen thee zee un?' urged the other, pointing to the reflection of the full moon in the water.

The travellers rode away, convulsed with laughter, and spread the tale. Bishop's Cannings men, up to their nonsense again. It was too good a story to be confined to Wiltshire. Verses were made up about it. One ballad contained the chorus:

> To zee thik dunder-haided coon
> A-reäking atter the shadder of the moon!

And Wiltshire people have been called Moonrakers ever since.

But the tale is in fact a subtle compliment. The travellers who accosted the 'moonrakers' were Excisemen, searching for smugglers, and the Bishops Cannings men had almost been caught with a cart-load of contraband brandy. When they had heard hooves approaching and guessed that it was the Excisemen on their rounds, they tipped their load into the pond. When all seemed clear, they started raking the brandy kegs out of the pond, but the Excisemen returned unexpectedly. Pretending to be drunk and feeble-minded was the best trick the smugglers could think of on the spur of the moment. Not a bad one, either. The Excisemen had their laugh, but the smugglers kept their brandy.

'The vlies be on the turmuts!' chuckle good Wiltshiremen, quoting the traditional march of the Wiltshire Regiment, 'but there bain't no vlies on we!'

For some unexplained reason All Cannings and Bishops Cannings are the butt of a large group of stories which hold them up to ridicule. Here is a selection.

At one time the people of Bishops Cannings decided to form a band. Someone remembered that there had been a band in the village previously, long ago, and a diligent search revealed assorted musical instruments in cottages, out-houses and even in the church vestry. It seemed a convenient place for the band to practise, so the musicians met there weekly until they felt confident enough to appear in public at the village fête.

Assembling in the vestry before their march around the village, they made a disconcerting discovery. Since the days of the previous band, a new door had been fitted to the vestry, and it was now too narrow to allow the big drum to pass through. So, it is said, the drummer sat in the vestry beating the big drum while the band marched around the village.

Another story is about the building of the church. The people of neighbouring villages noticed that two spires were being erected one bigger than the other. They laughed at the Bishops Cannings folk for being unable to build two of the same size, but they were told:

'Ah, we'll soon make the littl'un grow.'

So they piled loads of farmyard manure around the smaller

spire. When the heap began to sink they exclaimed, 'There! he be growin' up vine!'

Another story describes how Bishops Cannings people turned up in Devizes Market-place one evening. Someone in Devizes had told them a comet was due to appear, and they had come to town to see it. According to one version the entire population of the village are involved. Another says that it was only a carter, his wife and family, who came to watch an eclipse of the moon; they brought a rick ladder to place against their waggon, for a better view.

A gardener at Bishops Cannings vicarage saw a strange dog bite the handle of his wheelbarrow, and immediately he sawed off the handle, for fear of catching hydrophobia.

Another Cannings man, attempting to mend a barrel, instructed his small son to get inside and hold the sides steady while he finished the work. He was feeling very satisfied with the job when he heard the boy's voice coming from the bung-hole, 'How be I goin to get out veäther?' 'Oh, drattle the boy!' he exclaimed, 'I spose now I must knock in tother end.'

The following story of the Ticktoad, which was printed in the *Wiltshire Archaeological Magazine,* is in similar vein:

A shepherd coming home to dinner one day saw on the downs above Cannings a large watch. He had never seen a watch before and being afraid of the thing, thinking it was something dangerous as he could hear it ticking very loudly, he hurried to the village and told the sexton 'there were a great ugly beast up on the downs, and would he come and see it.' The sexton was a fat heavy man and said he could not walk so far but persuaded a couple of the villagers to wheel him up in a wheelbarrow. Two of them had their spades in their hands, and putting these in the wheelbarrow with the sexton, they made their way up to the spot, guided by the shepherd. On approaching the site they stopped and listened to the loud ticking of the watch. The sexton then said, 'Mates, just wheel I round him', which was done. 'Now wheel I round him again', and this was done a third time, when the sexton said, 'Mates, chuck I out', and crawling up nearer the 'beast' and listening for a minute he exclaimed, 'Mates, it be a dangerous ticktoad, so smash him up.' Whereupon the men with the spades smashed the watch and dug a hole and buried the pieces.

The same source supplies this tale:

> When I were walking whoam to Cannings tother night across the vields, ther come on a bit of a vog, but twer not so bad that I couldn't zee my way, and when crossing the second vield I seed out Jim coming t'ords I. But on getting a bit nearer he didn't zeem to me to be quite like our Jim, and when we met, why, dang me, twernt neither of us!

But I heard that story at Winterslow when I was a boy, and it contained no reference to Cannings.

A story given in *Folk-Lore* in 1900 sounds like a Cannings tale, though no location is supplied. A doctor was called to a man suffering from pleurisy and told the patient's wife to apply a blister to his chest. On returning, he was assured by the wife that the treatment had worked wonders, but he was surprised to find, on examination, no marks such as the application would cause. The wife explained, 'We hadn't got no chest, but he's got a good-sized box in that corner, so we clapp'd en on that.'

It is, in fact, a watered-down version of a much more scurrrilous tale still in circulation.

It could be that some of the tales told against Bishops Cannings were inspired by jealousy, for the village had at one time a high reputation, particularly for music. In his *Natural History of Wiltshire* John Aubrey records:

> Mr Ferraby, the minister of Bishops Cannings, was an ingenious man, and an excellent musician, and made several of his parishioners good musicians, both for vocall and instrumentall musick; they sung the Psalmes in consort to the organ, which Mr Ferraty procured to be erected.
>
> When King James I was in these parts he lay at Sir Edward Baynton's at Bromham. Mr Ferraby then entertained his Majesty at the Bush, in Cotefield, with bucoliques of his own making and composing; which were sung by his parishioners, who wore frocks and whippes like carters. Whilst his majesty was thus diverted, the eight bells (of which he was the cause) did ring, and the organ played on for state; and after this musicall entertainment he entertained his Majesty with a foot-ball match of his own parishioners. This parish in those dayes would have

challenged all England for musique, foot-ball and ringing. For this entertainment his Majesty made him one of his chaplains in ordinary.

Mr Ferraby organised a similar performance for Queen Anne, the wife of James I, at a place on Cannings Down on a later occasion, 'A copie of his song was printed within a compartment excellently well engraved and designed, with goates, pipes, sheep hooks, cornucopias, etc.'

15 Contemporary Folklore

FOLKLORE IS A LIVING and evolving thing, and probably the present generation has as lively an enthusiasm for the subject as at any time. It is not only that enthusiasts are collecting more assiduously than ever items of the old lore before they are forgotten; there is a widespread general interest in the way things used to be done.

In Wiltshire as in other counties Agricultural Preservation Societies or Clubs have sprung up, dedicated to preserving obsolete tools and machinery. Often younger farmers ask me, How did you plough a field in the days before tractors? What equipment did you have in your dairy? How was the sheep flock managed in the days of the great sheep farms on Salisbury Plain? Can you show us how to use a twig for water divining?

Then there are the recent memories. At Christmas old

photographs are brought out and we find reminders of the carnivals organised to raise money for a village hall; the harvest camps that helped with wartime harvests; Sunday School outings by waggon to farms four or five miles away; the earliest open charabancs that took us on excursions. We tell our children and grandchildren about them, just as my father told me about the village band, of which he was bandmaster, and about old sheep fairs and village cricket.

So much has happened in my lifetime. I saw the first cars enter Pitton, the first aeroplanes fly overhead, I have taken them in my stride, but I do sometimes find it hard to realise that even a bicycle is a comparatively recent invention and that my father, when he was young, possessed the first one in our village. At least, it was the first safety-bicycle. He used to tell of an old villager who had a penny-farthing on solid tyres on which he once rode the twenty miles to Southampton. He would talk about the Arctic winter of 1881, when there was a tremendous snow-storm in mid-January; but I think his stories are surpassed by my own recollections of the winter 1962/63, when the snow that fell on Boxing Day, 1962, was still on the ground in the second week of March.

New versions of the kind of tales told about Bishops Cannings still circulate, elements in them that mark them as modern. For instance, there is the old villager who complained that electricity cuts were not being fairly applied. 'I knows they baint', he declared. 'Just now when my missus were cooking my tea the cooker went off and all lights went out. There were we, setting in the dark, and the bally bus went by wi' all his lights on.'

Another story is of the old lady who was having difficulty with application forms for her widow's pension. At last she exclaimed in exasperation, 'Aw, drat it all! I wish my George were still alive. He'd have got it for I quick enough.'

A small boy in the primary class at the village school, asked why he thought the cow jumped over the moon, suggested, 'Praps there were a short circuit in the milking machine!' All these, which must have been invented within the past forty or fifty years, are enjoyed at Wiltshire village concerts, wherever someone can be found who can speak the Wiltshire dialect.

UFOs, or Unidentified Flying Objects, are another feature of modern Wiltshire folklore. Arthur Shuttlewood, features editor of the *Warminster Journal,* became interested in investigating local reports of such phenomena in 1964 and has since written several books on the subject, the first being *The Warminster Mystery*. In his second book, *Warnings from Flying Friends,* he writes:

> Up to Christmas of 1967 Bob Strong had seen 563 genuine UFOs, all but sixteen at night. Sybil Champion, our housewife observer, lynx-eyed in spotting the real and the 'phoney', had chalked up a total of 559. My humbler tally was 536 . . .
> Since February of 1966, Bob has taken no fewer than 3,523 camera shots of elusive spacecraft, of which only 101 have developed convincingly. However, we modestly claim that these comprise the finest collection of authentic pictures in the world, of their specialist kind . . .

Some of the witnesses that he mentions are:

> police, scientists, philosophers, medical specialists, senior teaching staff, astronomers, physicists, magistrates, local government officers, ministers of the Church, councillors, trade union officials, Army and Royal Air Force personnel, nursing staff and a hospital physiotherapist, college students, an aero-engine designer and the wife of a serving pilot . . . A number came deliberately to disprove the modest claims made by our trio of observers . . .

Cradle Hill, Warminster, seems to be the centre of these observations, and Mr Shuttlewood and his team of helpers have maintained a watch there on most nights. Many of the observations refer to phenomena in the sky. Says Mr Shuttlewood:

> UFOs take the vari-coloured shapes of glowing spheres, luminous pear-drops, ovular jewels that range from blood-red rubies to winking diamonds of flashing lights; from lustrous daytime pearls of shimmering surface to fiery emeralds that decorate the nocturnal heavens with fluorescent brilliance, transparent opals to dense white cigar aeroforms.
> Seen through a three-inch telescope at night, a hovering spacecraft is a glorious firefly of radiating colour changes,

pulsating from centre to outward edges in a continuous stream of flickering and living energy patterns, with white, amber, green, red and blue predominating.

The most common daylight variety is a gunmetal grey that sparkles with silver majesty when sunrays strike it through lurking fleecy clouds. Basic shapes are round, bell and long or torpedo . . .

Most of the UFOs recorded are small and have been observed from a distance, but, he adds: 'On Cradle Hill we see UFOs very low in altitude about once in every thirtieth clear night, on averge.' Since these observations were first made late in 1964 some of the objects are said to have landed, and Mr Shuttlewood and his team claim to have made contact with their crews. They are convinced that these are spacecraft from another planet, or planets, and *Warning from Flying Friends* enlarges on this theme.

Another West Country journalist and author, Mr. F. W. Holiday, in his book *The Dragon and the Disc*, describes two incidents from the Warminster district:

On 7 October, 1965, Annabelle Randall was driving her fiance, John Plowman, back to his home near Warminster. At 11.30 p.m. they approached a railway bridge near Heytesbury, where several fatal accidents have occurred.

As the car approached the bridge they saw a sprawled figure lying with its legs and feet on the road. Miss Randall managed to avoid them and stopped. It was found that the figure had vanished. A search of the road, the bridge and the surrounding area failed to reveal any trace.

At about 12.25 am. the girl set off alone on the return journey. Near the same bridge she saw a bright orange glow against an embankment. She describes it as a 'large orange ball' which suddenly shot across the road and took off into the sky.

Simultaneously, she became aware of a second round object, except that this one was dark and stationary. And walking along the road towards him came two figures wearing tight-fitting dark clothes and some sort of headgear. From the thighs downwards they glistened as if wet. The car almost ran them down as the now frightened driver kept going at top speed till she reached the town.

The following month a retired R.A.F. Group-Captain and his wife experienced a similar incident at 1.30 in the morning. As they approached Norton Bavant, which is only a mile from the location of the previous occurrence, they encountered a tall dark figure wearing some sort of mask. At the same instant, a second figure came staggering out of the hedge. This was the form of a naked, blood-covered youth, his face 'a pitiful sight', who looked like an accident victim.

The Group-Captain at once reversed, only to find that both figures had vanished . . .

Whatever the explanation of these phenomena, the Wiltshire UFOs add a new and fascinating element to the folklore of our county.

Here, to conclude, is a modern legend which comes from a letter written by Sir Michael W. S. Bruce to the *Evening Standard* on December 23rd, 1953:

Shortly before D-day I was sent on a course of instruction at Larkhill. Four of us went with an RAF W/O in a jeep to select suitable gunsites; we were coming up from the north towards the road which runs past Stonehenge, and between us and the road lay a small copse; suddenly we all saw a very small aircraft dive straight down into the wood and disappear in the trees; we raced the jeep up to give assistance; there was no sign of a crash – nothing – nothing flying away to the south. Suddenly I heard the W/O shout; he was standing white-faced before a large stone cairn commemorating the first death from an aeroplane accident in this country in 1912. It has been suggested that the apparition was that of Colonel F. S. Cody, pioneer of military aviation, who died nearby in his experimental aircraft. His was actually the first death in powered heavier-than-air flight; but the monument refers to Captain B. Loraine and S/Sergeant R. Wilson, who died in 1912, the first members of the RFC to do so.

Notes

1 *Stonehenge, Avebury and the Downland Barrows,* pages 15-25
STONEHENGE: Numerous publications. Especially useful are R. J. C. Atkinson, *Stonehenge* (1960); the article in the Encyclopedia Britannica (1972) by the same author, and a booklet *Stonehenge* (H.M.S.O., 1959) by Robert Newall.

The report prepared for King James I by Inigo Jones was never published, but later, in 1655, Jones's son-in-law, John Webb, published a book, *The Most Remarkable Antiquity of Great Britain, vulgarly called Stone-Heng, Restored,* in which he used some of the incomplete notes made by Jones.

GAFFER HUNT: John Smith, *Choir Gaur, the Grand Orrery of the Ancient Druids,* 1771.

THE DEVIL AND THE FRIAR: The story is widely known in Wiltshire and has been told to me on a number of occasions.

AVEBURY: John Aubrey (1626-1697), one of Wiltshire's earliest antiquaries, was born at Easton Piercy, near Malmesbury. His interest in Antiquities is said to have been first aroused by the sight of Avebury which he came upon unexpectedly, in 1648, when he was hunting. He writes: 'I was wonderfully surprised at the sight of these vast stones, of which I had never heard before, as also the mighty bank and graff about it . . . I left my company a while, entertaining myself with a more delightful indagation.'

An early edition of his *Natural History of Wiltshire,* edited by John Britton, was published by the Wiltshire Topographical Society in 1847 and reprinted in 1969.

DRUIDS: Dr. William Stukeley (1687-1765) wrote twenty books on Stonehenge, Avebury and other antiquities, the best known being *Stonehenge, a temple restored to the British Druids* (1740).

John Wood, of Bath, was an even more fanatical champion of the Druids. His contribution to the literature of Stonehenge was a book, *Choir Gaur, Vulgarly called Stonehenge, on Salisbury Plain, Described, Restored, and Explained,* published in 1747; *Encyclopedia Britannica,* 1972 ed, Vol. 7, pp. 706-7; T. G. E. Powell, *The Celts,* (1950) pp. 155-7.

WELSH TRIAD: Geoffrey Ashe, *From Caesar to Arthur,* 1960, p. 88.

SILBURY HILL, PALM SUNDAY: Rev. Charles Smith, *Wiltshire Archaeological and Natural History Magazine,* 1862, Vol. 7, p.180.

KING ZEL: Kathleen Wiltshire, *Ghosts & Legends of the Wiltshire Countryside,* 1973, p. 20-21, and personal communications.

MAN CRUSHED BY FALLEN STONE: Arthur Mee, *Wiltshire* (The King's England series), 1943, p.32; R. J. C. Atkinson, *Stonehenge and Avebury and Neighbouring Monuments,* 1959, p.45, suggests that the man was a barber-surgeon.

WEST KENNET LONG BARROW: Stuart Piggott, *The West Kennet Long Barrow,* 1962, *passim.*

PREHISTORIC SITES IN GENERAL: R. J. C. Atkinson, *Stonehenge and*

Avebury and Neighbouring Monuments, 1959; M. E. Cunnington, *Introduction to the Archaeology of Wiltshire,* 1938; Stuart Piggott, *Neolithic Cultures of the British Isles,* 1954. Gerald S. Hawkins, *Stonehenge Decoded,* 1966. Peter Fowler, *Wessex (Regional Archaeologies)* 1967.
BARROW GHOST STORIES: Kathleen Wiltshire, *Ghosts and Legends of the Wiltshire Countryside,* 1973, pp.2, 12, 21, 24, 25, 26.
MANTON BARROW: M. E. Cunnington, "Manton Burrow", *Wiltshire Archaeological and Natural History Magazine,* 1907, Vol. 35, pp.1-20.
CELTS: *Encyclopedia Britannica,* 1972 ed. Vol. 5, pp.146-152.

2 *The Hill Fairs,* pages 26-30
   Much of the information about the fairs that survived to within the last hundred years, and what went on at them, has come from personal communication, mainly from older farmers and shepherds.
WINDMILL HILL: R. J. C. Atkinson, *Stonehenge and Avebury and Neighbouring Monuments,* H.M.S.O. 1959, p. 54; see also, I. Smith, ed., *Windmill Hill and Avebury,* 1965, *passim.*
DEVELOPMENT OF HILL-TOP FORTIFIED EARTHWORKS: M. E. Cunnington, *An Introduction to the Archaeology of Wiltshire,* 1938, pp. 114-119; *Encyclopedia Britannica,* 1972 ed, Vol. 23, pp. 555-6; Grahame Clark, *Prehistoric England,* 1940, pp. 80-89; T. G. E. Powell, *The Celts,* 1963, pp. 86-91;
WILTSHIRE FAIRS: Mid-nineteenth century *Post Office Directories* contain much information about places and dates of now defunct Wiltshire fairs. The edition I have consulted is dated 1867; The quotation from Sir Richard Colt Hoare is from his *The History of Modern Wiltshire,* 1810-1821.
MARLBOROUGH: J. E. B. Gover, Allen Mawer & F. M. Stratton, *The Place Names of Wiltshire,* 1939, pp. 297-298; see also, Edith Olivier, *Wiltshire,* 1951, pp. 201-202.
MARLBOROUGH MAY FAIR: Pamela Street, *Portrait of Wiltshire,* 1971, p. 136, mentions that at Marlborough May Fair, seventy years ago, "the inhabitants joined hands and danced through the town, ending up by throwing various articles into the river and chanting, 'The tailor's blind and he can't see so we·will thread the needle.' The exact meaning of these words is obscure."

3 *Hill Carvings,* pages 31-35
Morris Marples, *White Horses and Other Hill Figures,* is a major source of information. Earlier writers are Rev. W. C. Plenderleath, *On the White Horses of Wiltshire and its Neighbourhood,* 1872, and *The White Horses of the West of England,* 1892; also, Sir Flinders Petrie, *The Hill Figures of England,* 1926. The concluding paragraph is an episode from my own experience.

4 *Festivals of May and Whitsun,* pages 36-48
Much of the information in this chapter is from personal experience.
WISHFORD OAK-APPLE DAY: I have attended these celebrations on several occasions and was once guest of honour at the festival luncheon. See also Edith Olivier, *Wiltshire,* 1951, pp. 244-246;

Pamela Street, *Portrait of Wiltshire*, 1971, p. 63; Ralph Whitlock, *Salisbury Plain*, 1955, pp. 152-156. Edith Olivier quotes fairly lengthy extracts from the main source document, *Sum of the Ancient Customs belonging to Wishford and Barford out of the Forest of Grovely*, 1566. Edward Slow, *Wiltshire Rhymes*, 1903, p. 150, gives an account of the Wishford customs in dialect verse: 'Tis Grovely; an ael Grovely; Thame shouten ael the day, Ta keep thic hankshint custom up, On girt Woak Apple Day.' A fine can be collected from any villager who fails to gather his green boughs in Grovely, and they must be brought home 'by strength of people'. Some time ago there was a controversy as to whether hand-carts and bicycles might be used, but the rules now allow them.

TRINITY SUNDAY: John Aubrey, ed. James Britton, *Remaines of Gentilisme and Judaisme*, 1686-87 (London 1881), pp. 136-138; also pp. 236-237.

VILLAGE WHITSUNTIDE CLUBS: personal recollections; also

EVERLEY: W. A. Edwards, *Everleigh, some Notes on its Story*, 1967, p. 26.

HARNHAM BESOM CLUB: *History of Harnham*, compiled in 1952-54 by Harnham Women's Institute.

LANDFORD CLUB: *Landford & Hamptworth Women's Institute Scrap Book*, compiled 1956. The Puritan whose fulminations are quoted was Thomas Hall, in *Funebriae Florae*, or *The Downfall* of May Games, 1660.

CUCKOO LORE, DOWNTON: from personal communications.

SALISBURY GIANT AND HOBNOB: ed. Hugh Shortt, *Salisbury*, 1972, pp. 129-132; also personal experiences.

ALDBOURNE DABCHICK: personal recollections of a BBC programme in which I was involved in the early 1950s. Also Ida Gandy, *The Heart of a Village*, 1975, pp. 16-17.

BELLS: Several of the horse-bells and other bells in my collection were cast by Robert Wells, the 18th century Aldbourne bell-founder. See also Ida Gandy, *The Heart of a Village*, 1975, pp. 33-38.

MERE: C. F. H. Johnston, 'Cuckowe King', *Folk-Lore* (1907), XVIII, pp. 340-1.

AMESBURY MAY DAY FEAST: Edith Olivier, *Moonrakings*, 1930, p. 54.

MAY DAY AT DURRINGTON: Edith Olivier, *Moonrakings*, 1930, pp. 59-60.

MAY GARLANDS AT SALISBURY & WILTON: J. P. Emslie, 'May Day' *Folklore*, 1900, XI, p. 216.

MAY DAY AT WOODFORD: Edith Olivier, *Moonrakings*, 1930, p. 64.

WHITSUNTIDE AT BERWICK ST. JAMES: Edith Olivier, *Moonrakings*, 1930, pp. 56-57; Also personal communications.

THE DUCK FEAST AT CHARLTON: Personal communications; Also ed. Hugh Shortt, *Salisbury*, 1972, pp. 134-135.

5 *More Festivals*, pages 49-79
Much of the information in this chapter is from personal recollections and communications.

SHROVE TUESDAY: Robert Chambers, *Book of Days*, Vol. 1, 1862, pp. 236-239. At Berwick St. James, Winterbourne Stoke and Stockton; Edith Olivier, *Moonrakings*, 1930, p. 57.

MARTINSELL HILL FAIR: Canon Jackson, 'The Vale of Warminster', *Wiltshire Archaeological and Natural History Magazine*, 1878, Vol. 17, p. 289.

SQUIRREL-HUNTING: *Teffont Women's Institute Scrap Book* 1956 mentions that it was a Teffont tradition to go squirrel-hunting on Palm Sunday. At Pitton squirrel-hunting was known as 'scuggy-hunting' and took place in Clarendon Woods on certain Sundays, but which dates are no longer remembered.

CLIPPING THE CHURCH: George Tyzack, *Lore and Legend of the English Church*, 1899, p. 71, contains information about Bradford-on-Avon and also places across the border in Somerset. Also at Crockerton and Hill Deverill, E. H. Goddard (ed.) "Wiltshire Folk Lore Jottings", *Wiltshire Archaeological and Natural History Magazine*, Vol. 50. p. 39.

ROGATIONTIDE: Personal experiences.

EVERLEY: W. A. Edwards, *Everleigh, Some Notes on its Story*, 1967, pp. 26-27.

BEATING THE BOUNDS AT MAIDEN BRADLEY: Edith Olivier, *Moonrakings*, 1930, p. 62.

CRICKLADE BARK FESTIVAL PLAY: Edith Olivier, *Moonrakings*, 1930, p. 88.

CALNE: A. E. W. Marsh, *A History of the Borough and Town of Calne*, 1903, p. 104.

EAST HARNHAM FEAST: *The History of Harnham*, A Women's Institute compilation, 1952-54, p. 11.

STOCKTON FEAST: Edith Olivier, *Wiltshire*, 1951, p. 240.

CRICKLADE LAMMAS FAIR: Edith Olivier, *Moonrakings*, 1930, p. 58.

CROCKERTON REVELS: John U. Powell, 'Folklore Notes for South-west Wilts', *Folk-Lore*, 1901, XII, p. 76.

BRITFORD FAIR: Personal recollections. See also, Ralph Whitlock, *Peasant's Heritage*, 1947, pp. 81-90.

HARVEST CUSTOMS: Personal recollections and communications, prior to 1940.

WILTON FAIR: Personal recollections and communications. See also Edith Olivier, *Moonrakings,* 1930, p. 41.

TENANCY CUSTOMS: Thomas Davis, *A General View of the Agriculture of Wiltshire*, 1811, pp. 29-34.

MICHAELMAS: Personal recollections and communications prior to 1940.

HIRING FAIRS: The derogatory statements are from Francis Heath, *Peasant Life in the West of England*, 1880, p. 69; also, Christina Hole, *English Custom & Usage*, 1941-42, pp. 94-95.

BONFIRE NIGHT: Personal recollections.

PIG-KILLING: Personal recollections.

BOY BISHOPS: ed. Hugh Shortt, *Salisbury*, 1972, p. 136; Joseph Strutt, *Sports and Pastimes of the People of England*, 1845, p. 346; John Brand, *Observations on Popular Antiquities*, 1900, pp. 228-234.

QUIDHAMPTON MUMMING PLAY: Edith Olivier, *Moonrakings*, 1930, p. 94.

OTHER MUMMING PLAYS: Amesbury, Cricklade, Horningsham, Maiden Bradley, Woodford; Edith Olivier, *Moonrakings,* 1930, pp. 54-66.

ALES: F. A. Carrington, 'Ancient Ales in the County of Wilts', *Wiltshire Archaeological and Natural History Magazine,* 1855, Vol. 2. pp. 191-204.

EVERLEY ALES: W. A. Edwards, *Everleigh, Some Notes on its Story,* 1967, pp. 25-26.

NEWNTON HERD ALE: John Aubrey, ed. James Britten, *Remaines of Gentilism and Judaisme,* 1686-87 (London, 1881) pp. 136-138; see also pp. 236-237.

MIDSUMMER: Eric Partridge and Jacqueline Simpson, *A Dictionary of Historical Slang,* 1972, p. 140. Joseph Wright, *The English Dialect Dictionary,* 1898, Vol. I, p. 468. John U. Powell, 'Folk-lore Notes from South-west Wilts', *Folk-Lore,* 1901, XII, pp. 72-73.

SHROVE TUESDAY: Alice Bertha Gomme, *The Traditional Games of England, Scotland and Ireland,* 1898, Vol. II, p. 230; J. B. Partridge, "Wiltshire Folklore", *Folk-lore,* 1915, Vol. XXVI, p. 211; John U Powell, 'Folk-lore Notes from South-west Wilts', *Folk-lore,* 1901, Vol. XII, p. 81.

PALM SUNDAY: J. B. Partridge 'Wiltshire Folklore', *Folk-lore,* 1915, Vol. XXVI, pp. 211-212. John U. Powell, 'Folk-lore Notes for South-west Wilts, *Folk-lore,* 1901, Vol. XII, p. 75.

CHRISTMAS: *This England,* 1974, VII, 21. John U. Powell, 'Folk-lore Notes from South-west Wilts', *Folk-Lore,* 1901, XII, p. 76.

NEW YEAR'S EVE: L. A. Law, 'Death & Burial Customs in Wiltshire', *Folk-Lore,* 1900, XI, p. 345.

PALM SUNDAY ON LONG KNOLL: Edith Olivier, *Moonrakings,* 1930, p. 62-63.

VILLAGE DANCING AT PITTON: Ralph Whitlock, *Peasant's Heritage,* 1947, p. 199.

CRICKLADE COURT LEET: Edith Olivier, *Moonrakings,* 1930, p. 59.

WISHFORD MIDSUMMER TITHES: Edith Olivier, *Wiltshire,* 1951, p. 251; Ralph Whitlock, *Salisbury Plain,* 1955, p. 150.

CRICKLADE LAMMAS FAIR: Edith Olivier, *Moonrakings,* 1930, p. 58.

PLOUGH MONDAY: Personal recollections.

6 *Local Customs,* pages 80-96

MERE: Edith Olivier, *Moonrakings,* 1930, pp. 63-64; T. H. Baker, 'Notes on the History of Mere', *Wiltshire Archaeological and Natural History Magazine* 1897, Vol. 29, pp. 319-321.

BERWICK ST. JOHN CURFEW BELL: Personal communication.

EVERLEY CRICKET: W. A. Edwards, *Everleigh, Some Notes on its Story,* 1967, p. 27.

LANDFORD CRICKET: *Landford & Hamptworth Women's Institute Scrap Book,* 1956, pp. 33-34.

WINTERSLOW CRICKET: *Winterslow by the W.I.,* 1956, p. 34.

WINTERSLOW BREAD & ALE ASSIZE: *Winterslow by the W.I.,* 1956, p. 4.

CRICKET AT PITTON & FARLEY: Personal reminiscences and communications.

HARVEST & HAYMAKING: *Landford & Hamptworth Women's Institute Scrap Book*, 1956, pp. 17-19.

CIDER-MAKING: Personal experience and communications.

WINTERSLOW TRUFFLE-HUNTERS: Personal communication. See also Ralph Whitlock, *Salisbury Plain*, 1955, p. 94., *Winterslow by the W.I.*, 1956, pp. 14-15.

MERE SQUATTERS: Edith Olivier, *Moonrakings*, 1930, p. 28.

SQUATTERS AT NOMANSLAND: *Landford & Hamptworth Women's Institute Scrap Book*, 1956, pp. 27-29, quoting *This Was My Village*, by Mrs. F. E. Winter (a prizewinning essay in a W.I. competition).

CHALK COB: Personal experience and communications.

DEWPONDS: Personal experience and communications. See also A. J. Pugsley, *Dewponds in Fact and Fable;* also *Winterslow by the W. I.*, 1956, pp. 23 and 32.

SHEEP BELLS: Personal experience and communications.

THROWING STICKS: Personal experience and communications.

SHEPHERDS' CROOKS: Personal experience and communications.

SKIMMETTING: Much information given me by my father. See also B. H. Cunnington, 'Moonrake Medley', *Wiltshire Archaeological and Natural History Magazine*, 1943, Vol. 50, pp. 278-280.

SMOCK WEDDINGS: G. S. Tyzack, *Lore & Legends of the English Church*, 1899, pp. 186-187.

7   *Wiltshire Characters and Personalities*, pages 97-109

ALFRED THE GREAT: John U. Powell, 'Folk-lore Notes from South-west Wilts', *Folk-Lore*, 1901, XII, p. 77.

KING LUD, KING INA & WODEN: Charles Thomas, 'Folklore from a Wiltshire village', *Folk-Lore*, 1954, LXV, pp. 165, 167. J. B. Gover, Allen Mawer and F. M. Stenton, *The Place-Names of Wiltshire*, Cambridge 1939, xiv, pp. 17, 318, 367-368.

JOHN RATTLEBONE: Arthur Mee, *Wiltshire*, 1943, p. 310.

SIR THOMAS BONHAM: John Aubrey, *Natural History of Wiltshire*, ed. J. Britten, 1847, p. 71, provides one of the earliest accounts. See also Edith Olivier, *Wiltshire*, 1951, pp. 248-249; Ralph Whitlock, *Salisbury Plain*, 1955, p. 156.

WILD DARRELL: Pamela Street, *Portrait of Wiltshire*, 1971 pp. 195-196; Ralph Whitlock, *Wiltshire*, 1949, p. 80; Arthur Mee, *Wiltshire*, 1943, pp. 92-93. For location of stile where Darrell was killed, see H. C. B., 'Moonrake Medley', *Wiltshire Archaeological and Natural History Magazine*, 1943, Vol. 50, pp. 280-281.

HIGHWAYMEN: Edith Olivier, *Wiltshire*, 1951, pp. 72-81. See also Ralph Whitlock, *Salisbury Plain*, 1955, pp. 181-182.

COOMBE BISSETT EXPRESS: Personal communication. Also *The History of Harnham*, compiled by the W. I., 1952-54, p. 18. There are also pictures of Mrs Rideout in Salisbury & Blackmore Museum.

CHALK LIGHTS: Personal communication.

ELIZA HARDING: Edith Olivier, *Moonrakings*, 1930, p. 47. Also personal communication.

DAVID SAUNDERS: Anon *David Saunders, The Shepherd of Salisbury Plain*, 1877.

DEAN OF IMBER: The inscription may still be seen on a roadside stone in the place indicated; the details of the story of the farmer's encounter with the highwaymen are from personal communication.

RUTH PIERCE: This story is from the inscription on the monument in Devizes Market-place.

MAUD HEATH: This is a well-known story. Her 'Causeway', with the inscriptions mentioned, still exists.

PURTON CHURCH: Personal communication.

THE OLD SARUM ARCHER: The story of the archer who shot the arrow from the ramparts of Old Sarum to the site of the new cathedral is found, briefly, in a number of publications; it also still circulates by word of mouth. E. E. Dorling, *A History of Salisbury*, 1911, p. 42, states that the arrow was shot by the bishop. Gleeson White, *The Cathedral Church of Salisbury*, 1896, recounts an alternative legend of the Virgin Mary appearing to the bishop in a dream and commanding him to build her new church in 'Myrfield'. He looked in vain for the place until one day he overheard a labourer mention it. The same author relates a tradition that the bishop at first tried to negotiate for a site with the Abbess of Wilton. His frequent visits to the Abbess for this purpose led an old sewing-woman to spread the rumour that the bishop wanted to marry the Abbess.

SWINDON: Personal communication. See also Pamela Street, *A Portrait of Wiltshire*, 1971, pp. 165-6.

CLARENDON PALACE: Personal communication from the 1930s, when, for a series of summers until the outbreak of war, I took part in the excavations.

8 *Witches, Giants and the Devil*, pages 110-115

WITCH AT WOOTTON RIVERS: Edith Olivier, *Moonrakings*, 1930, p. 86.

SOUTH WILTS WIZARDS: Edith Olivier, *Moonrakings*, 1930, pp. 80-82.

DEVIL AT LONGBRIDGE DEVERILL: John U. Powell, 'Folklore Notes from South-West Wilts', *Folk-lore*, 1901, XII, p. 74.

WITCH OF TIDCOMBE: E. R. Pole, 'Moonrake Medley' *Wiltshire Archaeological and Natural History Magazine*, 1943, Vol. 50, pp. 282-3.

LYDDIE SHEARS: Personal communications. Also Ralph Whitlock, *Salisbury Plain*, 1955, p. 225; *Winterslow by the W.I.*, 1956, pp. 27-28.

THE DEVIL & SILBURY HILL: *Folk-Lore*, 1913, XXIV, p. 524; L. A. Law, 'Death and Burial Customs in Wiltshire'; Robert Heanley, 'Silbury Hill', *Folk-Lore*, 1900, XI, p. 347.

GIANT AND HOBNOB: Personal experience. See also ed. Hugh Shortt, *Salisbury*, 1972, pp. 129-132.

CLEY HILL, SILBURY AND SIDBURY: Personal communications. See also Kathleen Wiltshire, *Ghosts and Legends of the Wiltshire Countryside*, 1973, pp. 20, 21; Pamela Street, *A Portrait of Wiltshire*, 1971, p. 129.

ARCHANGEL GABRIEL'S FEATHERS: Personal communications. Also S. Jackson Coleman, *Folk Lore of Wiltshire*, 1952.

WILLIAM OF MALMESBURY: The quotation is from *Chronicle of the Kings of England*, 1847 ed., p. 252.

9   *Funerals and Ghosts,* pages 116-134
Except where otherwise stated, the ghost stories in this chapter are recorded briefly by Kathleen Wiltshire, *Ghosts and Legends of the Wiltshire Countryside,* 1973, pp. 1-121, with additional details from other sources as listed below.
DEATH CUSTOMS: Personal experiences and communications.
PATTY'S BOTTOM: Edith Olivier, *Moonrakings,* 1930, p. 74.
DANERS: Personal communications. See also Edith Olivier, *Wiltshire,* 1951, pp. 102-3.
LONGLEAT: The Marchioness of Bath, *Longleat,* 1949, pp. 23-31, 37.
OLD COKER: S. Jackson Coleman, *Folklore of Wiltshire,* 1952. A few further details are given. The barrow around which he is heard galloping with his hounds is known as 'Gun's Church'. Chains rattle, and a ghostly horn sounds.
EDWARD AVON & THOMAS GODDARD: James Waylen, *A History of Marlborough,* 1854, pp. 553-558.
EXORCISM & BRADFORD-ON-AVON GHOSTS: S. Jackson Coleman, *Folklore of Wiltshire,* 1952, gives details of the exorcism of a ghost at Wyke House, Trowbridge, and of apparitions in the old Saxon church at Bradford-on-Avon.
DURNFORD DOWN GHOST: Personal communication. Also Edith Olivier, *Moonrakings,* 1930, p. 69.
PITTON STORIES: Personal communications.
PHILIPPS HOUSE: Personal communication.

10   *The Odstock Curse,* pages 135-146
Chief source – an unpublished chronicle by Hiram Witt, blacksmith of Odstock, written about 1870. Additional information from personal communications.

11   *The Poachers,* pages 147-151
General background; Ralph Whitlock, *Salisbury Plain,* 1955, pp. 244-246. Details from William Chafin, *Anecdotes and History of Cranbourn Chase,* 1818, *passim.*
CRANBORNE CHASE POACHERS: Personal communications. Also William Chafin, *Anecdotes and History of Cranbourn Chase,* 1818, pp. 9-41.
HARNHAM BRIDGE TOLLS: *The History of Harnham,* by Harnham Women's Institute, 1952-54, pp. 4-4.

12   *Animals, Plants & Traditional Remedies,* pages 152-173
Mostly from personal experiences and communications.
WITCH OF POTTERNE: B. H. Cunnington, 'Moonrake Medley', *Wiltshire Archaeological and Natural History Magazine,* 1943, Vol. 50, pp. 414-5.
WINTERSLOW LIONESS: Ralph Whitlock, *Salisbury Plain,* 1955, pp. 226-227.
BOAR AT WISHFORD: Ralph Whitlock, *Salisbury Plain,* 1955, p. 155; Edith Olivier, *Wiltshire,* 1951, pp. 249-250.
SABBATH-BREAKING AT BOREHAM: L. A. Law, 'Death and Burial Customs in Wiltshire', *Folklore,* 1900, XI, p. 347.

PIG LANE, BISHOPS CANNINGS: Kathleen Wiltshire, *Ghosts and Legends of the Wiltshire Countryside*, 1973, p. 34.

WITCHES' SCRAG TREE: Kathleen Wiltshire, *Ghosts & Legends of the Wiltshire Countryside*, 1973, p. 120.

MANDRAKE: Monica Money-Kyrle 'Mandrakes', *Folk-lore*, 1934, XLV, p. 192; C. J. S. Thompson, *The Mystic Mandrake*, 1934.

CHEESE: John Aubrey, *Natural History of Wiltshire*, ed. John Britton, 1847, pp. 105 and 115; see Val Cheke, *The Story of Cheese-Making in Britain*, 1959, pp. 15, 117-120, 134, 147-8, 194, 230.

13   *Some Wiltshire Songs*, pages 174-177
Personal recollections; also B. H. C. 'Moonrake Medley', *Wiltshire Archaeological Magazine*, 1943, Vol. 50, pp. 283-285.

14   *Local Humour*, pages 178-182
Personal communications and recollections.

WILTSHIRE MOONRAKERS: Postcards used to be on sale throughout Wiltshire with a reproduction of an old print of the 'moonrakers' and a brief version of the story, as souvenirs of Wiltshire. Edward Slow, *Wiltshire Rhymes for the West Countrie*, 1903, puts the story into dialect verse. See also Edith Olivier, *Wiltshire*, 1951, p. 232; Ralph Whitlock, *Salisbury Plain*, 1955, pp. 195-196; Pamela Street, *Portrait of Wiltshire*, 1971, p. 11.

THE CANNING STORIES: Edith Olivier, *Wiltshire*, 1951, pp. 232-236. A largish collection is printed in the *Wiltshire Archaeological and Natural History Magazine*, Vol. 50, 1943, pp. 278-286, 411-416, 481-485, under the title 'Moonrake Medley'. It includes all the stories recounted, except Bishops Cannings Band, which is from personal communication.

JAMES I AT BISHOPS CANNINGS: John Aubrey, *Natural History of Wiltshire*, ed. J. Britten, 1847, p. 109.

THE TICKTOAD: B. H. C. in 'Moonrake Medley', *Wiltshire Archaeological and Natural History Magazine*, 1943, Vol. 50, p. 413.

MR. FERRABY: John Aubrey, *A Natural History of Wiltshire*, ed. John Britton, 1847, p. 109.

15   *Contemporary Folklore*, pages 183-187
Personal recollections and communications.

UNIDENTIFIED FLYING OBJECTS: Arthur Shuttlewood, *The Warminster Mystery*, and *Warnings from Flying Friends;* also, F. W. Holiday, *The Dragon and the Disc*, 1973, pp. 213-214. Also *Evening Standard*, December 23, 1953.

Bibliography

W. ADDISON, *English Fairs and Markets,* 1953

GEOFFREY ASHE, *From Caesar to Arthur,* 1960

R. J. C. ATKINSON, *Stonehenge,* 1956, *Stonehenge and Avebury and Neighbouring Monuments,* 1959

JOHN AUBREY, *Remains of Gentilisme and Judaisme,* 1686-7 (London 1881) *Natural History of Wiltshire,* (ed. John Britton) 1847
  Wiltshire Collections, 1862
  Three Prose Works, (ed. John Buchanan-Brown), 1972

THE MARCHIONESS OF BATH, *Longleat,* 1949

A. G. BRADLEY, *Round About Wiltshire,* 1948

WILLIAM CHAFIN, *Anecdotes and History of Cranbourn Chase,* 1818

J. G. D. CLARK, *Prehistoric England,* 1963

S. JACKSON COLEMAN, *Folklore of Wiltshire,* 1968

M. E. CUNNINGTON, *An Introduction to the Archaeology of Wiltshire,* 1938

THOMAS DAVIS, *General View of the Agriculture of Wiltshire,* 1811

EDWARD E. DORLING, *A History of Salisbury,* 1911

W. A. EDWARDS, *Everleigh,* 1967
  Encyclopedia Britannica, 1972 ed.

J. B. GOVER, ALLEN MAWER & F. M. STANTON, *The Place-Names of Wiltshire,* 1939

Folklore, Myths and Legends of Britain (Reader's Digest), 1973

PETER FOWLER, *Wessex,* 1967

Folk-lore

IDA GANDY, *The Heart of a Village,* 1975

ALICE B. GOMME, *The Traditional Games of England, Scotland & Ireland,* 1898

JACQUETTA AND CHRISTOPHER HAWKES, *Prehistoric Britain,* 1958

GERALD S. HAWKINS, *Stonehenge Decoded,* 1970

FRANCIS HEATH, *Peasant Life in the West of England,* 1880

F. R. HEATH, *Wiltshire,* 1911

SIR RICHARD COLT HOARE, *Ancient History of Wiltshire,* 1812-1819
  Modern History of South Wiltshire, 1822-1844

CHRISTINA HOLE, *Haunted England,* 1940
  English Custom and Usage, 1941-42
  Witchcraft in England, 1945

F. W. HOLIDAY, *The Dragon and the Disc,* 1973

EDWARD HUTTON, *Highways and Byways in Wiltshire,* 1939

TOM INGRAM, *Bells in England,* 1954

R. L. P. JOWETT, *Salisbury,* 1951

MORRIS MARPLES, *White Horses and other Hill Figures,* 1949

ARTHUR MEE, *Wiltshire,* 1939

MURRAY'S *Handbook for Residents and Travellers in Wilts and Dorset,* 1899

ROBERT NEWALL, *Stonehenge,* 1959

EDITH OLIVIER, *Moonrakings,* 1930
  Country Moods and Tenses, 1942
  Wiltshire, 1951

ELLA NOYES, *Salisbury Plain,* 1915

SIR FLINDERS PETRIE, *The Hill Figures of England*, 1926
STUART PIGGOTT, *The West Kennet Long Barrow*, 1962
   Neolithic Cultures of the British Isles, 1954
REV. W. C. PLENDERLEATH, *On the White Horses of Wiltshire and its Neighbourhood*, 1872
   The White Horses of the West of England, 1892
Post Office Directories for the nineteenth century
T. G. E. POWELL, *The Celts*, 1958
A. J. PUGSLEY, *Dewponds in Fable and Fact*, 1939
ROWLAND W. PURTON, *Markets and Fairs*, 1973
DAVID SAUNDERS, *The Shepherd of Salisbury Plain, Anon*, 1877
HUGH SHORTT, (ed.), *Salisbury*, 1972
ARTHUR SHUTTLEWOOD, *The Warminster Mystery*, 1967
EDWARD SLOW, *Wiltshire Rhymes for the West Countrie*, 1903
A. C. SMITH, *The Birds of Wiltshire*, 1887
I. SMITH, (ed.) *Windmill Hill and Avebury*, 1965
JOHN SMITH, *Choir Gaur, the Grand Orrery of the Ancient Druids*, 1771
L. DUDLEY STAMP AND W. G. HOSKINS, *The Common Lands of England & Wales*, 1963
PAMELA STREET, *Portrait of Wiltshire*, 1971
JOSEPH STRUTT, *Sports and Pastimes of the People of England*, 1801
WILLIAM STUKELEY, *Stonehenge, a Temple restored to the British Druids*
BRIAN VESEY-FITZGERALD, *The Hampshire Avon*, 1950
JANE WAYLEN, *A History of Marlborough*, 1854
GLEESON WHITE, *The Cathedral Church of Salisbury*, 1921
JOHN WEBB, *The Most Remarkable Antiquity of Great Britain, vulgarly called Stone-heng, Restored*, 1655
RALPH WHITLOCK, *Peasant's Heritage*, 1948
   Salisbury Plain, 1955
   A Family and a Village, 1969
WILLIAM OF MALMESBURY, *Chronicle of the Kings of England*, 1847
KATHLEEN WILTSHIRE, *Ghosts and Legends of the Wiltshire Countryside*, 1973
WILTSHIRE ARCHAEOLOGICAL AND NATURAL HISTORY MAGAZINE, *from 1852 to present*
Women's Institute Scrap Books and village histories
JOHN WOOD, *Choir Gaure, Vulgarly called Stonehenge, on Salisbury Plain, Described, Restored, and Explained*, 1747
JOSEPH WRIGHT, *The English Dialect Dictionary*, 1898

Index of Tale Types

Folktales have been classified on an international system based on their plots, devised by Antti Aarne and Stith Thompson in *The Types of the Folktale*, 1961; numbers in this system are preceded by the letters AT. Some local legends were classified by R. Th. Christiansen in *The Migratory Legends*, 1958, and his system was further developed by K. M. Briggs in *A Dictionary of British Folktales*, 1970-1; these numbers are preceded by ML, and the latter are also marked by an asterisk.

Motif Index

A motif is an element that occurs within the plot of one or several folktales (e.g. 'cruel stepmother'). They have been classified thematically in Stith Thompson's *Motif Index of Folk Literature*, 1966; the numbers below are taken from this, together with E. Baughman's *Type and Motif Index of the Folktales of England and North America*, 1966.

General Index